Nobody paid much attention to Roland and the group assembled on Highway 151. After all, it looked like a relatively harmless gathering of baby boomer gun enthusiasts repeating fairly common complaints about the government. What nobody realized was that this ragtag group was part of something much larger. Not even Roland knew that in at least a dozen other states across the country, citizens were simultaneously forming their own militias.

A new social movement was emerging.

Two thousand miles from Sea World in San Antonio, John Trochmann and his family initiated the Militia of Montana in a tiny town just south of the Canadian border. On April 17, Tom Cox launched the Oregon Militia. Two days later, another group started a militia in San Diego. At the same time others were getting started in Alabama and Arizona. Armed groups calling themselves militias have sprung up before, but in the spring of 1994 the new militias appeared spontaneously and simultaneously from coast to coast.

THE RIGHT TO BEAR ARMS:

THE RISE OF AMERICA'S NEW MILITIAS

By Jonathan Karl

HarperPaperbacks
A Division of HarperCollins*Publishers*

HarperPaperbacks   *A Division of* HarperCollins*Publishers*
10 East 53rd Street, New York, N.Y. 10022

Cover photograph by REX USA LTD.
Cover photograph of Branch Davidian Compound by AP/Wide World Photos

First printing: December 1995

Printed in the United States of America

HarperPaperbacks and colophon are trademarks of HarperCollins*Publishers*

❖ 10 9 8 7 6 5 4 3 2 1

To Maria

ACKNOWLEDGMENTS

I owe an enormous debt of gratitude to my editors at the New York *Post*, especially Stuart Marques, Marc Kalech, and Ken Chandler. Without their encouragement, generous support, and patience, this book, quite simply, would not have been possible. Together with publisher Martin Singerman and a talented staff, they have turned the *Post* into a hard-hitting, irreverent, and street-smart newspaper that consistently beats out its staid and often snooty competition. They have made me part of the transformation, and for that I am extremely grateful.

In writing this book, I attempted to immerse myself in the world of the average militia member; I explored the Internet, tuned into patriotic talk shows on short-wave radio, attended militia meetings and rallies, and interviewed militia members throughout the country. The process was time-consuming and exhausting, but the unwavering support of my advisors, colleagues, friends, and family made it possible to complete this project within the ambitious timeline set by Geoff Hannell at HarperCollins, who somehow had faith in my ability to produce the book on time.

No support was more crucial than that of my wife,

Maria, who provided critical editorial advice and helped keep me organized and focused. A trio of informal editors (and mentors) gave me instant feedback and constructive criticism on virtually every page I wrote, as soon as I wrote it: Andrew Krauss, Howard Shaff, and, of course, my mom.

I probably wouldn't have even attempted this book if it weren't for Douglas Kennedy, the gutsy journalist who convinced me to work for the *Post* in the first place. As one of the best in the business, he also taught me the art of investigative reporting. *Post* columnist Andrea Peyser provided advice and encouragement, and I also benefited from the reporting of others at the *Post,* including William Neumann, Jeff Simmons, and Al Guart.

Post librarian Laura Harris provided an immense amount of critical research assistance. Laura and her first-rate staff, especially Nicola Pullen, pulled together volumes of newspaper and magazine articles, books, television and radio transcripts, and court records.

A major challenge in researching this book was penetrating the often secretive world of the militias. This would have been nearly impossible without the help of a few key militia members who granted me hours and hours of interview time and spread the word to others that I could be trusted with their stories. Among those who were particularly helpful were Brad Alpert of the 51st Militia in Missouri, Jon Roland of the Texas Constitutional Militia, Ken Adams of the Michigan Militia, Arizona militia and gun-rights activist Ernest Hancock, and others who helped me on the condition that I would not reveal their names. I also benefited from the work and assistance of those who study the militia movement, including the researchers at the Anti-Defamation League and Chip Berlet of Political Research Associates in Boston.

I am indebted to several others who gave me feedback and encouragement, including Wayne F. Karl, Allan Karl, Scott Alexander, Sal and MaryAnn Catalano, Wendy Fisher, Piotr Madej, Deroy Murdock, Brian Brown, Richard Dawson, Mike Dayton, Bill Hoffman, Michael Hechtman, David Seifman, my editor Jessica Lichtenstein, and my agents Lynn Chu and Glen Hartley. Thanks, and cheers.

TABLE OF CONTENTS

THE RIGHT TO BEAR ARMS:

THE RISE OF AMERICA'S NEW MILITIAS

TEA-PARTY TIME IN AMERICA

A well regulated Militia being necessary to the security of a free State, the right of the people to keep and bear Arms shall not be infringed.

—U.S. Constitution, Second Amendment

It's dangerous to be right when the government is wrong.

—Voltaire

A crowd of uneasy Americans, most of them gun owners, crammed into St. John's Church in Richmond, Virginia. There were rumors of war in the air—not a foreign war, but a war fought by the government against its own citizens. Those who couldn't fit inside the church listened from outside.

A thirty-year-old lawyer rose to speak. Calmly at first, he warned that the worst of the rumors were true: The government was preparing an attack on the citizens. It was amassing a great force, conspiring to take guns away from the citizens, and readying a plan to enslave the people.

Arousing fear—and paranoia—in all who could hear him, his voice grew louder as he called for action against this conspiracy. Able-bodied citizens, he implored, must prepare for a war against the forces of our outlaw rulers, against our government.

"An appeal to arms and the God of Hosts is all that is left us," he bellowed. "The war is inevitable—and let it come! I repeat it, sir, let it come!"

At the frenzied crescendo of his speech, he appeared possessed. An eyewitness described it this way: "The tendons of his neck stood out white and rigid, like whipcords. His voice rose louder and louder, until the walls of the building and all within them seemed to shake and rock in its tremendous vibrations. Finally, his pale face and glaring eyes became terrible to look upon. Men leaned forward in their seats with their heads strained forward, their faces pale and their eyes glaring like the speaker's. When he sat down, I felt sick with excitement."[1]

And so did the others. Less than a month later, some of those influenced by the speaker's call for violent action took matters into their own hands. The consequences were deadly. On April 19, there was an explosion; nearly three hundred people were left dead or injured.

But the speaker knew what was coming; he endorsed it; he was willing to pay any price.

At the close of his fateful speech, he roared, "Is life so dear, or peace so sweet, as to be purchased at the price of chains and slavery? Forbid it, almighty God! I know not what course others may take; but as for me, give me liberty or give me death!"

The date was March 23, 1775. The speaker was Patrick Henry. And the explosion that followed on

---

[1] As quoted in William Safire, ed., *Lend Me Your Ears* (New York: W. W. Norton, 1992), p. 85.

April 19, 1775, was a gun fired in Lexington, Massachusetts, the first shot of the American Revolution—the shot heard around the world.

Today the sounds of revolution are once again in the air—rumors of war, disdain of leaders, fear of government. Across America, citizens in virtually every state have spent part of the past couple of years preparing for civil war, arming themselves for the next American Revolution. Tens of thousands are stockpiling ammunition and emergency supplies, coordinating field and firearms training, and creating sophisticated communications networks and surveillance teams to monitor government actions.

These men and women see themselves as modern-day Patrick Henrys. They quote his speeches. They know the history of the citizens' militias he encouraged to fight the British during the Revolutionary War. They know their Constitution and its Second Amendment guarantee of the right to keep and bear arms.

The rumblings have been heard across America for a while and are growing stronger—witness the swelling ranks of tax protesters, county-rights advocates and home-schoolers, estimated to be five million strong. The patriot movement—as the ranks of those intensely alienated from the federal government call themselves—is made up largely of working-class, middle-aged Americans who are convinced that the spirit of 1775 is upon us again. The patriots of two centuries ago fought a government in London that they believed imposed unreasonable taxes, trampled on their rights, and was unresponsive to their needs. Today's self-styled patriots shake their fists at the government in Washington, D.C., which they believe imposes unreasonable taxes, tramples on individual freedom, and is unresponsive to their needs.

As Louisiana congressman Bill Tauzin put it, "It's tea-party time in America."

At the Boston Tea Party of 1773, American colonists protested British rule and unfair taxes by dumping tea into Boston Harbor; today's self-styled patriots demonstrate their distaste with governing authorities in similarly creative ways. Consider these scenes from the front lines of the patriot movement:

• In Nye County, Nevada, politicians have declared local laws superior to federal laws. When the National Forest Service closed off an area to logging, the county commissioner climbed onto a bulldozer and plowed through the barricade as hundreds of citizens cheered. The U.S. Department of Justice estimates that seventy counties nationwide have followed Nye County's lead, most of them in California. Other observers put the number of counties at as many as three hundred.

• In Roundup, Montana, five fugitives armed with assault rifles barricaded themselves in a cabin owned by the Internal Revenue Service, which had taken control of the site a year earlier for tax evasion. The fugitives have issued a "citizens' declaration of war" and offered bounties on local officials, saying they should be hung. "When the Feds asked what they could do, I said, 'Send me a tank.' People think I'm joking, but I'm not. We need help," said Musselshell County prosecutor John Bohlman.

- In Concordville, Pennsylvania, Carris Kocher works with her five-year-old daughter to make "Second Amendment aprons" that feature a little pocket designed to hold a handgun. "We've all got to be able to protect ourselves, even Abigail," she explains with a smile.

- In Graham County, Arizona, Sheriff Richard Mack refused to enforce the Brady bill, which requires a five-day waiting period for handgun purchases. He took his challenge to court and won. Would Mack enforce any gun-control laws passed by Congress or the state legislature? His answer is firm: "No. I swore an oath to uphold the Constitution of the United States and the Constitution says, 'No gun control.'"

- In 1993 and 1994, Congress passed two landmark gun-control laws: a ban on the manufacture of assault weapons and the Brady bill. Also in 1993 and 1994, a record number of guns was sold in the United States—more than five million each year. The Brady bill and the ban on assault weapons created what in essence was a panic; people rushed out and purchased more firearms, especially handguns and assault weapons. There are now more than sixty-five million civilian gun owners in America, possessing over two hundred million working firearms.

- Nationwide, seven million working Americans refuse to pay income tax each year, according to the Internal Revenue Service. Many have disavowed their Social Security numbers and

consider the IRS an outlaw organization that
confiscates the earnings of citizens to finance an
unjust government.

The militias are the armed wing of this modern
patriot movement.

Armed rebellion and resistance are certainly not
new in America. American history is rich with stories
of everyday citizens who took up arms to fend off
injustice, whether real or imagined. In the 1960s,
groups on the radical left, such as the Weather
Underground and the Black Panthers, turned to violent resistance to combat what they considered an
oppressive American system. In the 1970s and 1980s,
right-wing race-based groups such as the Order and
Posse Comitatus took up arms in the name of white
supremacy and tax protest.

But the militia movement of the 1990s represents a
new and remarkably widespread social movement.
Most militias now seen across the country were
formed after 1993, and although some of the movement's leaders have long been active in alternative
politics, most of the rank and file are new to the
world of political activism.

Unlike some of the paramilitary groups that preceded them, they are motivated as much by fear as by
hate. Their mantra is self-defense. They have formed
not to wage a campaign of terror but to defend themselves from a terror campaign they believe is already
being waged by their own federal government.

The ranks of the militias are made up of factory
workers, veterans, computer programmers, farmers,
housewives, small-business owners. The most shocking thing about these "paramilitary extremists" is how
normal they are. They are your neighbors.

But in another sense, many members of America's new militias live in a parallel universe, where civil war is already being waged by tyrants within the federal government.

An intense fear drives them. They stockpile food, first-aid supplies, guns, and ammunition. The various conspiracy theories that swirl through the movement see doom in America's near future: war, martial law, and one-world dictatorship. They see danger signs everywhere: gun-control laws, overreaching federal law enforcement officers, and U.S. involvement in the United Nations. They know what is coming because they have researched it intensively, exhaustively documenting government atrocities and the erosion of their rights. They don't rely on CNN, ABC News, or the *Chicago Tribune* for their information. They tune in shortwave radios to alternative talk shows, read "intelligence reports" posted on computer bulletin boards and the Internet, and exchange information through extensive fax networks.

Sadly, the federal government has too often given these people reason to be afraid while at the same time feeding their conspiracy theories. If it's tea-party time in America for the new patriots, events such as the 1993 federal siege of the Branch Davidian compound in Waco, Texas, serve as the Boston Massacre, which in 1770 helped galvanize American colonists to prepare for the Revolutionary War.

Real government conspiracies, such as the Iran-contra affair and the BCCI scandal, give an aura of credibility to the most paranoid conspiracy theories. When rumors of clandestine operations, deception, and intrigue at the highest levels of government turn out to be true, anything seems possible. Iran-contra was a real scheme—orchestrated right out of the basement of the

White House by top advisors to the president—in which officials secretly sold weapons to Iran in a bid to both free hostages and funnel the proceeds to anti-Communist guerrillas fighting thousands of miles away. In the surreal pinnacle of this scheme, the president's national security advisor actually gave a birthday cake shaped like a key to the Ayatollah Khomeini. As Michael Kelly wrote in the *New Yorker,* "The unfolding revelations of Iran-contra gave a great and lasting boost to conspiratorial thinking every-where in America: If this impossible scenario was true, then nothing was beyond credibility."[2]

Although they fear civil war is coming, the leaders of citizens' militias insist that it will be the govern-ment, not the militias, that fires the first shot. They are organized for self-defense, not to overthrow the government, and certainly not to resort to terrorism. "We're like a giant neighborhood watch," explains John Trochmann, the cofounder of the Militia of Montana and one of the most influential voices in the movement.

But this neighborhood watch is convinced that war is coming, and coming soon.

"Make no mistake about it: People are angry. The only thing that stands between some of the legislation being passed here and all-out war is time," Ohio mili-tia leader James Johnson told a U.S. Senate hearing on the militias.

Shortly after this Senate hearing, Ray Southwell of the Michigan Militia put it more starkly: "If the truth is not told, Congress will pass legislation that will drive this country into civil war."

---

[2] Michael Kelly, "The Road to Paranoia," the *New Yorker,* June 19, 1995, p. 69.

The legislation Southwell and the others fear would give more power to federal law enforcement agencies (such as the FBI and the Bureau of Alcohol, Tobacco, and Firearms) to investigate and crack down on groups such as the citizens' militias. They also fear gun-control measures and any efforts to take outlawed guns out of the hands of citizens.

Samuel Sherwood of the United States Militia Association in Blackfoot, Idaho, sees civil war unfolding if there is a crackdown on militias and further government actions such as the siege in Waco. These actions, he says, will provoke an unorganized and terroristic response by dangerous elements within the militia movement who will seek vengeance. "The flash point is rising so high that we are going to see not just another Waco, but two or three major disasters. After that—talk about Oklahoma City! I don't know where all the federal buildings are, but I wouldn't walk into one for the next two years.

"The government actions are spawning a thousand Irish Republican Armies, with everybody believing differently, but everybody ready to battle the government."

Following the April 19, 1995, bombing of the Alfred P. Murrah Federal Building in Oklahoma City, militia leaders such as Samuel Sherwood, Ray Southwell, and James Johnson found themselves vilified in the national news media, blamed for the most deadly terrorist act in American history. They had nothing to do with the actual bombing, but it was revealed that suspects Timothy McVeigh and Terry Nichols had attended militia meetings in Michigan.

All militia members were thus pronounced *guilty*

by attendance—one step removed even from guilt by association. Neither McVeigh nor Nichols was a member of any known militia, although both received extensive training in the art of warfare as members of one of the world's largest military organizations: the U.S. Army.

Like militia leaders, McVeigh and Nichols were appalled by the federal siege of Waco and intensely distrustful of the federal government. They moved in the same world of gun shows, conspiracy theories, and tax protest. In a 1992 letter to his hometown newspaper, the *Union-Sun & Journal* of Lockport, New York, McVeigh wrote: "We have no proverbial tea to dump; should we instead sink a ship full of Japanese imports? . . . Is a civil war imminent? Do we have to shed blood to reform the current system? I hope it doesn't come to that! But it might."

But every militia leader in the country condemned the bombing. They insisted that their groups were formed for defense, not terrorism.

Even President Clinton, riding popular sentiment, tied the Oklahoma bombing to citizens' militias when, in a major speech shortly after the attack, he condemned the militia movement: "There is nothing patriotic about pretending that you can love your country but despise your government. . . . How dare you call yourselves patriots and heroes?"

The penchant for far-out conspiracies, for stockpiling arms, and for extreme paranoia is certainly a dangerous mixture, but the militia movement isn't the only resting place for "conspiracists."

Whether or not it has anything to do with a militia group, the Oklahoma bombing leaves a number of haunting questions unanswered: How many self-styled patriots are ready to take Patrick Henry's words to heart? How many truly believe, as Patrick Henry did in March 1775, that the war is already being waged, that it's time to fire back?

"THEY KILLED MY WIFE! THEY KILLED MY SON!"

2

I thought I'd have to run out of the cabin and start shooting. I figured I was going to die and I wanted to take a few of them with me.

—*Sixteen-year-old Sara Weaver*

The ultimate enemy of any people is not the angry hate groups that fester within, but a government itself that has lost its respect for the individual.

—*Defense attorney Gerry Spence*

Don't call Randy Weaver paranoid.

His worst fears about the government have already come true.

A former Green Beret soldier during the Vietnam War, Weaver is a separatist in every sense of the word. In 1983, he withdrew from modern society, moving his family from Iowa to a remote section of northern Idaho thirty miles from the Canadian border. He built a cabin on the side of a nearly inaccessible mountain called Ruby Ridge, a couple of miles outside Naples, a tiny town with a population of less than a hundred. His twenty-by-twenty-five-foot plywood hut had no running water, no electricity, no telephone. But hidden away in the thick pine forest on Ruby Ridge, Weaver thought he would be left alone, free to live off the land and raise his children in his own way. His new home was only a hundred yards from a trout stream, and the evils of modern life seemed a million miles away. No one, he thought, could touch him.

In the summer of 1992, Weaver's remote dreamland would be invaded by the largest, deadliest federal force ever seen in Boundary County.

Weaver's problems with federal authorities dated back to 1989, when he sold Kenneth Fadeley two of his shotguns. Fadeley wanted the shotgun barrels sawed off, to make them a quarter of an inch shorter than the legal length. Fadeley turned out to be an undercover agent for the federal Bureau of Alcohol, Tobacco, and Firearms (ATF). The ATF offered Weaver a choice: become an ATF informant or face an illegal weapons charge. They asked Weaver to infiltrate the Aryan Nations—to be a government plant at the neo-Nazi group's headquarters in Hayden Lake, Idaho. A white separatist, Weaver had been spotted at the hate group's whites-only compound in Hayden Lake, which is less than a hundred miles from Ruby Ridge.

When Weaver refused to become an informer, he was arrested and ordered to appear for trial on February 19, 1991, in Moscow, Idaho. The judge changed the date to February 20, but a letter sent to Weaver incorrectly ordered him to appear on March 20. When Weaver didn't appear, the federal judge issued a bench warrant for his arrest and a grand jury indicted him for failing to appear before the court.

Afraid that he was going to be thrown in jail and ripped away from his family, Weaver refused to surrender. He turned his tiny cabin into a well-armed, if flimsy, fortress for himself, his wife, Vicki, and their children, Rachel, Sara, and Samuel.

"I feel I have no choice but to stay here if I want to keep my family together," Weaver told a local reporter at the time.

His defiance won him supporters throughout Boundary County, the Pacific Northwest, and beyond. Even people who didn't agree with his white-separatist views admired his challenge to federal authority and his refusal to leave his family.

But the authorities believed this slight man—five feet seven inches tall and weighing barely 120 pounds—was extremely dangerous. A look at his rickety cabin made the idea seem laughable, but the Feds had reasons to believe Weaver was a real threat. A few years earlier a highly secretive, underground splinter group of the Aryan Nations called the Order had plotted a frightening terror campaign of assassinations and bombings. In 1984 the Order pulled off a $3.8 million heist of a Brink's armored car and assassinated Denver talk show host Alan Berg. In November 1984, the group's leader, Robert Jay Matthews, was killed after a fierce firefight with FBI agents in Washington State. Weaver had no ties to the Order, but he had been seen at the Aryan Nations headquarters and the authorities clearly feared that he too was capable of murder; Randy Weaver, authorities feared, could be another Bob Matthews.

The federal government's fear of Weaver faced off against Weaver's fear of the federal government, setting the stage for a tragic series of events that would give birth to the new militia movement. Weaver himself never joined a militia, but he was destined to become the movement's first martyr, its rallying cry.

As Weaver and his family held out in their plywood cabin, nobody took Weaver's cause to heart more than Carolyn and John Trochmann.

Every few weeks the Trochmanns would make the hour-and-a-half trek to Ruby Ridge from their home in Noxon, Montana. They would bring food, ammunition, and other necessities. Randy had run out of money, so he would try to repay them by offering whatever gift he could; at one point he gave John a broken-down snowmobile.

Carolyn Trochmann had met Vicki Weaver a year earlier at a "family day" event held at the Aryan Nations' headquarters. The Trochmanns' son Caleb had become close friends with the Weavers' oldest daughter, Sara. In October 1991, Carolyn was at Ruby Ridge to help Vicki the day after she gave birth to her third daughter, Elisheba.

The baby girl was born while the world closed in on her father. Weaver was still a fugitive for ignoring his court date, and the U.S. Marshal Service had put him on their ten-most-wanted list. Spending hundreds of thousands of tax dollars, they encircled Randy's cabin, beginning an elaborate, high-tech surveillance operation.

The U.S. Marshal Service installed $130,000 worth of long-range, solar-powered reconnaissance cameras. They took aerial photographs of Weaver's cabin and had them studied by the Defense Mapping Agency. They intercepted Weaver's mail. Using night-vision equipment, they maintained twenty-four-hour surveillance. They had psychological profiles done; they even knew the menstrual cycle of Weaver's teenage daughter Sara and planned an arrest scenario around it.[1]

The U.S. marshals also bought property next to

---

[1] David Nevin, "It Could Happen to Anyone," *Washington Post*, July 18, 1993.

Weaver's so that an undercover agent could build a cabin, pose as a neighbor, and, they hoped, befriend Weaver and lure him away from his slipshod fortress.

But Randy wouldn't fall for that. He didn't trust anybody anymore. In April 1992 he told the Trochmanns to stay away; he suspected them of being government informants. About the only person he still associated with was twenty-three-year-old Kevin Harris, a family friend from Oregon who often lived with the Weavers.

On the morning of August 21, Deputy U.S. Marshal Arthur Roderick led a six-man team to the wooded area surrounding the Weaver cabin. Outfitted in full camouflage, with paint on their faces, the men carried automatic weapons. It was Roderick's twenty-fourth mission to the cabin area. This time he caught the attention of Weaver's golden retriever, Striker.

Barking wildly, Striker ran down the hill from the cabin, toward the agents. Fourteen-year-old Sammy Weaver and Kevin Harris followed after the dog.

A shot rang out. A single bullet sent Striker's crimson intestines flying in Sammy's direction. His dog was dead. In a panic, the boy fired his gun in the direction of the camo-clad officers.

"Sammy, get back up here!" Randy yelled from the cabin after he heard the gunshots.

Weaver's lawyer, Gerry Spence, describes what happened next.

"The little kid says, 'I'm coming, Dad.' Those were the last words he ever spoke. And he's running, with his back to the officers. And they open fire on this little kid. They shoot off his arm first of all; it was dangling there like a bloody sausage. And then they shoot him in the back. And he falls."

Randy Weaver's only son was shot in the back.

Seeing Sammy dead, Harris fired in the direction of the officers and, according to the U.S. marshals, killed William F. Degan. Harris then ran back to the cabin while the marshals scrambled down the hill to their command post. Later that day, Randy, Vicki, and Kevin went to retrieve Sammy's body, bringing it to a shed behind the cabin to prepare it for burial.

Back at the command post, officials reported that Degan had been killed in a lengthy firefight. But for nearly a day, they didn't reveal that Sammy had been killed.

Later the marshals' office retracted the story of the massive firefight, but not before word zoomed to FBI headquarters in Washington, D.C. The FBI's elite paramilitary Hostage Rescue Team was immediately dispatched to Ruby Ridge. By then, nearly four hundred federal, state, and county law enforcement officers surrounded Weaver's plywood cabin. At this time, the top two agents on the operation—Richard Rogers and Larry Potts—changed the standard FBI rules of engagement, which stipulate that an officer may use deadly force only when he, or a third person, is in imminent danger. Potts and Rogers put out different orders: Shoot any armed male on sight, whether or not he poses an immediate danger.

With the rules set and hundreds of officers on the scene, FBI snipers surrounded the cabin. They were backed up with two armored personnel carriers and two Idaho National Guard helicopters.

The next day, Randy Weaver, unaware of the massive force that now encircled Ruby Ridge, ventured outside his cabin with his daughter Sara and Kevin Harris to see Sammy's body. As they approached the body, FBI sharpshooter Lon Horiuchi fired. A West Point graduate, Horiuchi is considered one of the FBI's best shots. His shot hit Randy in the shoulder.

Randy, Sara, and Kevin dashed back to the cabin, while Vicki, with ten-month-old Elisheba in her arms, stood in the doorway yelling to them to hurry.

Horiuchi's next shot hit the wrong target. He later testified that he was following Harris through his rifle's scope, aiming slightly ahead of the running man.

Horiuchi pulled the trigger just as the three got to the doorway. The bullet struck Vicki in the temple, sending her limp body to the ground as baby Elisheba remained cradled in her arms. Fragments of that fatal bullet passed through Vicki's skull and wounded Harris. Randy ran up and took the screaming baby from Vicki's arms. He lifted his wife's head to find that half her face had been blown away. In horror, he and his daughter Sara stretched the dead woman's body on the cabin floor, covering it with a blanket.

The siege went on for another nine days, and during that time Vicki's body remained on the floor of the cabin, slowly decomposing before the eyes of her three surviving children. No more shots were fired after Vicki was killed because the survivors stayed huddled inside the cabin, out of the sight of the snipers' scopes. But the psychological torture was just beginning.

"How's the baby, Mrs. Weaver?"

"Good morning, Mrs. Weaver. We had pancakes for breakfast. What did you have?"

"Come out and talk to us, Mrs. Weaver."

The FBI, which claimed not to have known Vicki was dead until days after she'd been shot, taunted

Randy Weaver and his children with these words
after Vicki was killed.

The FBI waited three days to announce Vicki's
death, but beginning on the first day of the siege,
Weaver's supporters had gathered at the police roadblock two miles from his cabin on Ruby Ridge. They
set up a vigil and harangued law enforcement officials. The whole Trochmann family came over from
Noxon and set up tents. John Trochmann guided jour-
nalists through the woods to show them the extent of
the paramilitary buildup facing down Weaver's tiny
plywood cabin. As the siege, which lasted eleven
days, went on, Carolyn Trochmann drove back to
Noxon each night, returning the next morning with
spaghetti and bread to feed the growing encampment
of Weaver supporters.

The crowd that gathered below Ruby Ridge caught
the first glimpse of the patriot movement's new hero
and, more important, its new villains. The men on the
other side of the police barricades wore uniforms
bearing the initials *FBI* and *ATF*. When the shooting
of Vicki Weaver was finally made public, the image of
these officers as cold-blooded murderers was indeli-
bly ingrained in the minds of people such as the
Trochmanns. It would be another year until
Trochmann started the Militia of Montana, but the
stage was set.

"Our own military was across that line," Carolyn
said, crying as she recounted the story. "People who
swear an oath to protect the people of this country
were up there killing their own people."

The protesters carried signs with a new slogan for
the patriot movement: *Your Family Could Be Next.*

Some of the people at the pro-Weaver encampment shared his white-separatist views. The führer of

the Aryan Nations, Richard Butler, made the trip up from Hayden Lake, and five skinheads were arrested for trying to smuggle assault rifles up to Ruby Ridge. But most of the protesters were simply everyday citizens outraged to see such a massive federal force battling an unassuming man and his family hiding in a tiny, handmade cabin.

On the eleventh day of the siege, Randy Weaver gave himself up. He had been promised a good lawyer, and he got one: the flamboyant Gerry Spence of Jackson Hole, Wyoming, one of the premier defense lawyers in America.

Spence was an unlikely defender for a cagey, white-separatist loner. His courtroom attire is unconventional: a ten-gallon Stetson cowboy hat, cowboy boots, a buckskin jacket with fringe. And his politics are diametrically opposed to Weaver's: "I'm so far left, I'm almost pink," Spence says. He's a champion of liberal causes, and as much as he deplored Randy Weaver's views, he saw the siege as a dangerous display of government power.

"I met Randy Weaver in jail on the evening of his surrender," Spence wrote in his book *From Freedom to Slavery*.

> His eyes had no light in them. He was unshaven and dirty. He was naked except for yellow plastic prison coveralls, and he was cold. His small feet were clad in rubber prison sandals. In the stark setting of the prison conference room he seemed diminutive and fragile. He had spent eleven days and nights in a standoff against the government, and he had lost. His wife was dead. His son was dead. His

friend [Kevin Harris] was near death.
Weaver himself had been wounded. He
had lost his freedom. He had lost it all. [3]

Immediately after taking the case, Spence was
attacked by his liberal friends, who charged that he
was lending credibility to white supremacy. He thun-
dered back, "To the same extent that Randy Weaver
cannot find justice in this country we, too, will be
deprived of justice. At last, my defense of Randy
Weaver is a defense for every Jew and every Gentile,
for every black and every gay who loves freedom and
deplores tyranny." [4]

In addition to the original firearms violations,
Weaver and Kevin Harris were charged with the murder of federal marshal William Degan. Nobody was
charged with the killing of Vicki and Sammy Weaver.

The trial began in June 1993. Assistant U.S. attorney
Kim Lindquist presented the prosecution's case: "This
is a case of resolve on the part of Weaver and Harris to
defy laws to the point of using violence. This whole
thing is a tragedy. . . . The cause was the resolve of
the Weaver family, and that translates into murder."

By the time of the trial Weaver had already become
an underground folk hero of the patriot movement
for his stand against the Feds, and a martyr for the
price he paid. The courtroom was packed with many
of his supporters. They were horrified to hear the
family's resolve blamed for murder.

---

[3] Gerry Spence, *From Freedom to Slavery: The Rebirth of
Tyranny in America* (St. Martin's Press: New York, 1993),
p. 11.

[4] Ibid.

Tapping into the raw emotion of the courtroom, Spence, standing three feet from the jury, bellowed the response Weaver's supporters wanted to hear: "The theme of this case is to demonize Randall Weaver and make him into an ugly, hateful, spiteful person"—as he spoke he banged on his lectern—"so that they could cover up the murder of a boy shot in the back and a woman shot in the head."

The jury agreed. Spence rested Weaver's case without calling a single witness. Weaver was acquitted of the most serious charges, including the original firearms charge. Judge Edward J. Lodge took a step unusual in criminal cases and fined the prosecution $3,200 for delays in providing critical evidence to defense attorneys.

Weaver was the one on trial, but the proceedings revealed deadly misconduct on the part of federal law enforcement officials. The FBI compounded its folly during the siege by tampering with evidence for the trial. Two FBI agents, Greg Rampton and Larry Wages, testified that the FBI had staged photographs taken at the scene of the shoot-out: They planted bullet shells on Ruby Ridge at the site of the first shoot-out and photographed the scene. Federal prosecutors presented the photos in court as evidence.

An extensive Justice Department investigation of the FBI's conduct during the Weaver siege yielded a 542-page report that faulted the bureau for criminal misconduct, but Attorney General Janet Reno did not make the report public. FBI director Louis Freeh censured twelve agents for "inadequate performance, improper judgment, neglect of duty, and failure to exert proper managerial oversight." But the stiffest penalty Freeh doled out was thirteen days' unpaid leave, and that was for only four of the agents. The

FBI has inflicted harsher penalties on agents who
drove their children to school in Bureau cars. The
senior official on the Weaver siege, Larry Potts,
received only a letter of censure and was later promoted to the number two spot in the FBI, acting
deputy director. Three years after the standoff, in
August 1995, Freeh took further action, suspending
Potts and three other agents.[5]

The Justice Department report, a copy of which
made it into the hands of *Legal Times,* described the
shot that killed Vicki Weaver with chilling detail: "No
call-out or surrender announcement followed the first
shot. The subjects were never given a chance to drop
their arms to show that they did not pose any threat.
The subjects simply did what any person would do
under the circumstances. They ran for cover."[6]

The report also came down hard on Potts's decision to allow the changed rules of engagement, calling
the move a violation of the Fourth Amendment: "This
inquiry finds that the Rules expanded the use of
deadly force beyond the scope of the Constitution and
beyond the FBI's own standard deadly force policy."

---

[5] Weaver sued the federal government shortly after his
trial. In August, the Justice Department settled the case,
giving $3.1 million to Weaver and his three daughters.
The government admitted no wrongdoing in the settlement, but Justice Department spokesman Carl Stern said,
"The settlement reflects the loss to the Weaver children of
their mother and brother. For the department, there was a
genuine desire to take a step toward healing the wounds
the incident inflicted."

[6] "Verbatim: DOJ Probes the Wreckage at Ruby Ridge,"
Legal Times, March 13, 1995, p. 15.

The future members of the militia movement would take lessons from the Weaver case that would become some of the central tenets of the militia movement:

- The government will stop at nothing to enforce gun-control laws.

- FBI agents are capable of cold-blooded murder—even killing a mother holding a ten-month-old baby in her arms.

- Government agents will use undercover informants to entice law-abiding citizens into breaking the law.

- The government will tamper with evidence to cover up wrongdoing.

- Even after getting caught breaking the law, federal agents are not held accountable for their actions.

After serving out the remainder of his eighteen-month sentence, Weaver moved to Grand Junction, Iowa, to raise his surviving children. His showdown with the Feds on Ruby Ridge helped give birth to the militia movement, but, true to his separatist beliefs, he has joined no groups. In a rare interview a month after the Oklahoma bombing, Weaver told *Time* magazine:

> I'm not a joiner. I don't belong to the militia or any other group. I have my own take on things. Hell, I'm really not even a

Christian. But I get calls all the time from
the militia and other groups to come talk. I
can't now. But if I do, I think I would only
last a few speeches. They would find out I
don't really agree with them either.

Less than a year after the Weaver showdown,
another FBI-ATF siege arising out of firearms violations energized the patriot movement. The siege of the
Branch Davidian compound in Waco, Texas, was more
widely reported than the showdown at Ruby Ridge. It
lasted longer and it was deadlier, but the April 19,
1993, firestorm in Waco only confirmed the worst
fears spawned by the events at Ruby Ridge. The citizens' militias were on their way.

WACO: THE SHOT HEARD ACROSS AMERICA

3

It was the people who ran their cult compound at Waco who murdered their own children.

—President Bill Clinton

We are at war, right now, make no mistake about it.

—Indiana militiawoman Linda Thompson

The horrible inferno in Waco, Texas, on April 19, 1993, consumed seventy-four people. Seventeen of them were children younger than eight years old.

Federal authorities went after David Koresh and the Branch Davidians for the same reason they initially went after Randy Weaver: alleged violations of federal gun laws. Weaver was charged with possessing illegally sawed-off shotguns; the Branch Davidians were suspected of converting AR–15 semiautomatic rifles into illegal machine guns. But the Weaver siege took place in the thick pine forest of northern Idaho, more than two miles from the nearest television camera. In contrast, the sight of the burning Branch Davidian compound reached millions of people who had never heard of Randy Weaver.

The Waco firestorm, and the fifty-one-day standoff that preceded it, was beamed via satellite around the world. Those who died in the blaze were members of an obscure religious sect called the Branch Davidians. An offshoot of the Seventh-Day Adventist Church, the Branch Davidians believed that "End Times," the apocalypse described in the biblical book of Revelation, were coming soon. Their leader was David Koresh, a thirty-three-year-old former member of a rock-and-roll band who believed he was the second Messiah. Over half of the 130 Branch Davidians living in Waco in February 1993 were ethnic minorities: Forty-five were black, and another twenty-five were either Hispanic or Asian.

The drama started at 9:00 A.M. on February 28, 1993. Eighty armed and uniformed officials of the federal Bureau of Alcohol, Tobacco, and Firearms (ATF) stormed the grounds of Mount Carmel, the church and home of the Branch Davidians in Waco. The ATF code-named the raid "Operation Showtime." Their aim: to serve an arrest warrant on David Koresh and search the compound for a suspected vast arsenal of illegal weapons.

Gunfire quickly erupted as the agents swarmed the compound. An unrelenting exchange of high-powered ammunition went on for more than ten minutes. By the time the smoke cleared, four ATF agents and six Branch Davidians were dead.

It's unclear who fired the first shot on February 28, but the Branch Davidians refused to surrender and the fifty-one-day standoff began.[1] The FBI's elite

---

[1] After a seven-week trial of the eleven surviving Branch Davidians, a San Antonio jury could not reach a decision on who fired the first shot. At one point, the ATF said it had a videotape that proved the first shots came from inside the compound; but that tape, if it exists, has never been publicly shown.

Hostage Rescue Unit—the same team used in the Randy Weaver showdown—was called in. Within days more than seven hundred law enforcement officers—from the FBI, the ATF, the Waco police, the National Guard, the Texas Rangers, the U.S. Customs Service, and the McClennan County sheriff's office—were on the scene.

At the end of the second week of the siege, the FBI, frustrated by Koresh's unwillingness to surrender, started to pursue a plan of "stress escalation": They cut off electricity to the compound, set up loudspeakers to blare loud music and other noises (including Tibetan chants and the sound of rabbits being slaughtered), and shone searchlights on the building at night. They hoped to fragment the group's unity through sleep deprivation and psychological pressure.

But the effort seemed only to strengthen the resolve of the Branch Davidians. Inside the compound, David Koresh and his followers apparently believed the forces arrayed against them were the forces of the devil. Without some sign from God, they did not believe surrender to be an option. They chose to wait.

After nearly two months of a tense standoff, Attorney General Janet Reno gave the order to put an end to the siege with a final, all-out assault on the compound. She later said she based her decision on a number of factors, the most significant being unsubstantiated reports that Koresh was abusing the children inside the compound.

With Reno's go-ahead, the FBI led its forces into action. Shortly after 6:00 A.M. on April 19, two M–60 tanks began poking holes into the side of the compound and introducing CS gas into the building (CS gas is a particularly potent form of the tear gas sometimes used by law enforcement to disperse crowds). By shooting the canisters into the Waco compound, the FBI hoped to force the Branch Davidians to run outside.

The Texas winds seemed to blow most of the CS gas away, so after several hours the federal authorities escalated the attack. Four Bradley armored vehicles joined the effort, firing 40-mm canisters of CS gas through the windows.

An officer's voice blared through loudspeakers aimed at the compound:

"David, you have had your fifteen minutes of fame. . . . Vernon [Koresh's given name] is no longer the Messiah. Leave the building now. You are under arrest. The standoff is over."

Shortly after noon, smoke could be seen coming from the second-story windows. Within minutes the entire building was engulfed in flames. The uncontrollable inferno dominated the skyline; only nine Branch Davidians managed to escape. The charred remains of most of the women and children were found huddled together in a concrete storage area near the kitchen.

The cause of the fire is a matter of incredible controversy.

Former attorney general Ramsey Clark, a left-wing activist who has represented such clients as LaRouche and a former Nazi concentration camp guard, alleged that the April 19 inferno was caused by the CS gas canisters fired into the compound. Clark has filed a civil lawsuit against the government on behalf of several Branch Davidian survivors.

The FBI maintains that the Branch Davidians started the fire themselves as part of a mass-suicide pact, but the nine survivors deny their group had any intention of committing suicide. The truth may never be known because most of the evidence was destroyed in the fire.

For millions of people who watched the horrible blaze on television, it was the sad culmination of a government action against a bizarre cult that committed mass suicide. But a more terrifying message found its way into the hearts and minds of future militia leaders: The federal government is at war with its own citizens.

For them, the April 19 date of the Waco firestorm had special significance.

Exactly 218 years earlier—on April 19, 1775—British soldiers marched to Lexington, Massachusetts, to take action against illegal firearms. The British "redcoats" aimed to destroy weapons stockpiled by the colonists and to arrest two dangerous colonial rabble-rousers, John Hancock and Samuel Adams. But on Lexington Green, the redcoats ran into the Minutemen, colonial militiamen armed to defend themselves and their weapons supply. The first musket shot fired, immortalized in American history books as "the shot heard around the world," galvanized militia patriots throughout the thirteen colonies and launched the American Revolution.

For some, Waco had more in common with the battle on Lexington Green than just the date. Like the battle of Lexington, the Waco firestorm was a wake-up call: The redcoats are coming, only this time they are wearing dark uniforms bearing the initials *FBI* and *ATF*.

"Waco was the second shot heard round the world. It woke us up to a very corrupt beast," explained Russell Smith, the Dallas commander of the Texas Constitutional Militia.

"The Waco siege really did it for me. The Feds came after these people to get their guns. Who would be next? I knew there was something deeply wrong in America," said Brad Alpert, a forty-two-year-old computer operator and member of the 51st Militia in Kansas City, Missouri.

Smith and Alpert, like thousands of other Americans, responded by joining a militia. They vowed to be well armed and prepared for the next government attack.

How did so many red-blooded American patriots come to decide that the death of a bizarre cult meant it was time to stockpile weapons and form citizens' militias? In part, the answer lies with one woman: Linda Thompson.

An Indianapolis lawyer, Thompson is an odd pioneer for a movement widely considered to be made up of "angry white males." In 1991 she first made headlines as a pro-choice attorney; she sued the mayor and the police chief of Chamblee, Georgia, for failing to protect a women's clinic from antiabortion protesters. A lawyer who knew her at the time said, "She always came across as a very feminist, pro-woman civil-rights lawyer." In an interview with *NUVO,* an alternative newsweekly in Indianapolis, she called antiabortion activists "fanatics" and "no-choicers." She compared the Pro-Life Action League to the Ku Klux Klan and said she was "deeply committed to the fight to preserve a woman's right to choose."

"Two years ago, I was a fairly ordinary person," Thompson said in the spring of 1995.

Thompson's "ordinariness" began to fade when she first heard of the Randy Weaver standoff. Horrified by the government's actions, she says she resolved to get involved if another situation arose.

Her moment came in March 1993, as the Waco siege intensified. "I had decided to go to Waco and file a petition for David Koresh," Thompson later wrote in an article distributed through her computer network. "In this case, we were asking the Court to order the FBI to observe David Koresh's legal rights and also to allow an attorney in to see him (none had been allowed in at that time)." Thompson offered her legal services to Gary Hunt, a Florida-based land surveyor and ultraconservative journalist and activist who had been serving as David Koresh's representative since the beginning of the siege.

Hunt was part of a growing crowd that journeyed to Waco to protest the siege. He had developed a fax network that transmitted daily updates to a growing group of Americans that didn't trust what they read about Waco in the newspapers. Hunt's network worked like a phone tree: He faxed material to a list of people around the country, who would each in turn fax it out to others, and on and on. The fax system became the American Patriot Fax Network and continues to flourish as an important communications tool for militia activists around the country.

Hunt and Thompson worked together for about a week when they decided, in Hunt's words, "to walk into the compound to see what the cops would do." As they approached the FBI roadblock Thompson started handing out press releases announcing their plan. But the two had a falling-out and Thompson headed back to Indianapolis.

In less than two weeks, Thompson rushed back to Waco with a new plan. The siege was entering its sixth week, and the crowd of protesters now numbered in the hundreds. Perhaps sensing the opportunity to attract a following, Linda Thompson the lawyer became Linda Thompson the militant activist.

She issued a call to arms in the form of a press release. "JOIN US! The Unorganized Militia of the United States of America will assemble, with long arms, vehicles (including tracked and armored), aircraft, and any gear for inspection for fitness and use in a well-regulated militia, at 9:00 A.M. on Saturday, April 3, 1993, on Northcrest Drive, off I–35."

Before the militia assembly took place, Hunt approached Thompson and approximately thirty people assembled at a Dairy Queen in Waco.

"I asked her if she'd join our peaceful demonstrations, and she said, very loudly, 'Gary, you're a government agent!'"

Hunt issued a "Call for Peace" and in a communiqué addressed to "My Fellow Patriots" urged anyone coming to Waco to come unarmed and to "use some good Common Sense." But Thompson's "first assembly of the unorganized militia" didn't live up to its billing anyway. A couple dozen protesters haphazardly brandished unloaded weapons in a perfectly legal protest against the Waco siege. There was no aircraft, no armored vehicles. Thompson wore military camouflage and waved her AR–15 assault rifle as news photographers snapped pictures.

Why she decided to call out the "unorganized militia" is unclear, but whatever the reason, her call was premature. It would be close to a year before the militia movement took root nationally.

Thompson postponed militia organizing for a while and set out on a new mission: "I vowed then I would make it my personal responsibility to expose the truth to America," she said.

After months of exhaustive research, she began to

tell the story of Waco as a wicked case of government murder, conspiracy, and cover-up. She didn't need the mainstream media to get her story out; Thompson relied on alternative ways to disseminate information. She established a computer bulletin board service and produced her first commercial videotape: *Waco: The Big Lie*.

In the months following the Waco siege, most political observers—liberals and conservatives—came to agree that the federal action in Waco was a colossal, and deadly, mishap. Even the Treasury Department issued a scathing critique of its Bureau of Alcohol, Tobacco, and Firearms. The report faulted the ATF for pursuing the raid in the first place and for making "false or misleading pronouncements" in the days that followed. The head of the agency was forced to resign and the operation's commanders were demoted.

But in *Waco: The Big Lie* and its sequel, *Waco II: The Big Lie Continues*, Thompson constructed her theory about the siege. It's a theory that alleges more intrigue, deception, and malfeasance than do even the strongest critics of the federal government's actions in Waco.

In the films, Thompson displays "uncut" video footage of the siege that she insists proves a dastardly conspiracy. Some of her more alarming "findings" include:

- The government used flame-throwing tanks to start the fire.

- The four ATF agents killed in the initial assault were murdered by other ATF agents, not by Branch Davidians, who she says did not fire a single shot.

- As the blaze began, federal agents entered the compound and gunned down Branch Davidians, including children, who were trying to escape.

Thompson's videos became underground bestsellers, reaching thousands of people across the country who reasonably had doubts about the official version of the Waco siege. She popularized a view now believed by most in the militia movement: The Branch Davidians didn't commit mass suicide and were deliberately slaughtered by the ATF and the FBI. Oklahoma bombing suspects Timothy McVeigh and Terry Nichols were reported to be among those who watched Thompson's videos. The videos raised legitimate questions about the operation, but they also went further, fueling the paranoid idea that the government has declared war on its citizens.

They also turned out to be quite profitable. Bob Brown, editor of *Soldier of Fortune* magazine, estimates that Thompson has made over $300,000 on her Waco videos in less than two years. The videos, which Thompson sells for $19.95, were aggressively marketed in *Soldier of Fortune* and through a growing network of alternative media arising out of the patriot movement.

Thousands of people gobbled up Thompson's videos because they thirsted for an alternative to the Waco story told in their daily newspapers and on the evening news. Intense distrust of the mainstream media—including CNN, TV network news, major daily newspapers, the Associated Press, and so on—had become almost as important a part of the patriot movement as intense distrust of government. The events in Waco fueled this hatred of the media.

During the fifty-one days of the Waco siege, the

mainstream media covered the unfolding drama from a press holding area two and a half miles from the Mount Carmel compound. Daily government briefings drove the media coverage, providing sound bites for the evening and headlines for the daily newspapers. Reporters, with the help of government sources, also delved into the dark side of the Branch Davidians, portraying David Koresh as a crazed egomaniac, sexual deviant, and child abuser. Far less examined were the actions of the FBI and the ATF.

A patriot protest song about Waco by Carl Klang, a logger and musician from Oregon, put it this way:

> Yesterday I sold my TV set
> Stopped my subscription to the *Times*
> To me, it's plain to see the media
> Was an accomplice to these crimes

Thompson turned Klang's song, called "Seventeen Little Children," into a music video, further helping to fuel anger about the federal government's actions in Waco. An emotional folk-rock ballad about the children who died in the April 19 firestorm, the song puts the blame for the children's deaths squarely on the shoulders of Attorney General Janet Reno and President Bill Clinton.

> Seventeen little children
> All so helpless and so small
> Died a senseless death of gas and flames
> How many names can you recall?

> Seventeen little children
> Don't it make you wonder why?

Seventeen little children
How could they deserve to die?

Maybe we should stop and ask ourselves
If we become so blind
Will seventeen little children finally open
  up your eyes?

How did you sleep last night, Bill Clinton?
Did you feel their pain?
Seventeen little children
Cried out and perished in the flame

Attorney General Janet Reno
I accept your offer to resign
How can you stand for law and order now
When you won't answer for your crimes?[2]

The growing suspicion that the media had presented a one-sided portrait of the Waco siege created
an opening for Thompson. She responded in full
force. After the Randy Weaver incident in 1992, she
had set up a self-styled "think tank" in Indianapolis
called the American Justice Federation (AJF). After
Waco, she turned the AJF into an underground
media mecca, a full-blown and high-tech American
samizdat press operation. Thompson churned out
thousands of copies of her videotapes, newsletters,
stickers, audiocassettes, and books. Working with
her husband, Al, she developed a computer network
and twenty-four-hour electronic bulletin board service that distributed her message—and hawked her

[2] Reprinted with the permission of Carl Klang, P.O. Box
217, Colton Oregon, 97017.

goods—to a potential audience of millions of computer users.

Thompson was contributing to the development of shadow media, a sophisticated alternative to CNN and the daily newspapers. The shadow media reach a nationwide audience of alienated Americans by using diverse tools: underground newspapers, fax machines, shortwave radio, the Internet, videotapes, public-access TV, and the established publications of extreme right-wing groups such as the Liberty Lobby and the John Birch Society.

There was no room in the shadow media for Rush Limbaugh, Newt Gingrich, Oliver North, or any of America's other prominent conservatives. Limbaugh was disliked because he had praised Attorney General Janet Reno for taking strong actions against the Branch Davidians. And conservative Republicans such as Gingrich were seen as coconspirators with liberal Democrats. Virtually everybody in power was distrusted or even despised.

Emboldened by the Waco firestorm, the shadow media sent out an almost apocalyptic message: The government is launching a war against free-minded citizens. For the pessimistic, the Waco siege was evidence that the war had already started. For the optimistic, war lies ahead in the near future and can be won only if citizens prepare to defend themselves.

THE BIRTH OF A MOVEMENT

4

The Armed Militia says, "The legislatures and the courts are corrupt; and, God helps those who help themselves. Aim at the tyrant's head." Their methods are Militant Protest, Show of Arms and Colors, Visible Strength, Fearful Determination.

—Manual of the
Michigan Militia Corps

We no longer have the confidence in local law enforcement to protect us. If there is another Waco, we will look to the militia to defend the innocent, and the outcome may be quite different.

—Jon Roland, founder,
Texas Constitutional Militia

McDonald's and Sea World stand sentry over an unfinished stretch of Highway 151 in northern San Antonio. It's an unlikely place to start a second American Revolution.

And the crowd that gathered on that dusty roadway on April 19, 1994, seemed unlikely heirs to the legacy of Paul Revere and Patrick Henry. About fifty men and women and a dozen children milled around, showing off their firearms and talking about government corruption. Most of the adults were in their forties and fifties; one man was well into his eighties. Almost all were veterans of the military or law enforcement. They wanted to start something big, something historic. They carried an impressive array of firearms, ranging from pistols to assault rifles. One guy showed up in a replica of the Minuteman uniform worn exactly 219 years earlier by the colonial militiamen during the Battle of Lexington and Concord. He carried his colonial-era musket—antique, but still fully operational. Another donned the uniform worn by the Confederate soldiers during the Civil War. The rest wore either military camouflage fatigues or everyday civilian clothes.

The Paul Revere of this gathering wore a dark gray all-weather suit. A computer programmer from San Antonio, he was a veteran of Ross Perot's 1992 presidential campaign and, more important for the purposes of this meeting, a self-taught historian of the U.S. Constitution. His name was Jon Roland. For the first ten minutes, Roland hid in the bushes with a video camera as the others came together and gathered in a circle. He had feared a violent government crackdown on the militia and was prepared to document any brutality with his video camera. When it became clear a crackdown wasn't going to happen, Roland emerged from the bushes and addressed the crowd.

"Several weeks ago, somebody suggested that we declare this day, April nineteenth, the Right to Bear Arms Day," Roland said as others nodded in agreement.

"I said no. Every day is Right to Bear Arms Day. Let's dedicate this day, this year and every year, as Militia Day."

Like a professor giving a lecture to an introductory

history class, Roland explained the significance of
April 19.

"Now we all know what happened at the Branch
Davidian compound near Waco last year on April
nineteenth. And it was on April nineteenth, 1775,
that the militiamen of Lexington and Concord fought
off an attempt by British authorities to disarm them,
and thereby started the War of Independence. April
nineteenth is also the anniversary of the Warsaw
ghetto uprising, when courageous Jews defied their
Nazi oppressors. It's the approximate date of the
siege at Wounded Knee in South Dakota."

With the sounds of revolution once again in the
air, Jon Roland and the others talked about increasing
threats to freedom in America. A "shadow government" controls most of the world, Roland told the
people assembled. "They will take away our rights if
we let them. And they will start by taking away our
guns." The best way to prevent this, he said, was to
activate the Texas Militia, an armed group of citizens
dedicated to defending freedom.

Nobody paid much attention to Roland and the group
assembled on Highway 151. After all, it looked like a
relatively harmless gathering of baby-boomer gun
enthusiasts repeating fairly common complaints about
the government. What nobody realized was that this
ragtag group was part of a much larger social movement. Not even Roland knew that in at least a dozen
other states across the country, citizens were simultaneously forming their own militias.

A new social movement was emerging.

Two thousand miles from Sea World in San
Antonio, John Trochmann and his family initiated the

Militia of Montana in a tiny town just south of the
Canadian border. On April 17, Tom Cox launched
the Oregon Militia. Two days later, another group
started a militia in San Diego. At the same time others were getting started in Alabama and Arizona.
Armed groups calling themselves militias have sprung
up before, but in the spring of 1994 the new militias
appeared spontaneously and simultaneously from
coast to coast.

The most ambitious militia founding took place on
April 29, 1994, in the woods of northern Michigan. A
cabal of thirty armed men met in secret, elected a
commander, and made plans for their first public
meeting. Two weeks later, the group assembled in the
village of Pellston, Michigan (population 580). Three
dozen armed men gathered in a village park, less than
a hundred yards from a Little League baseball game.
In full battle regalia, their faces smeared with black
and green paint, they inaugurated the First Brigade of
the Northern Michigan Regional Militia.

They took the militia oath:

> I do solemnly swear that I will support and
> defend the Constitution of the United
> States against all enemies, both foreign
> and domestic; that I will bear true faith
> and allegiance to the same; and that I will
> obey the orders of those appointed over
> me, for conscience sake; So Help Me God.

Led by the pastor of Calvary Baptist Church,
Norman Olson, and his deacon, Ray Southwell, they
brandished semiautomatic rifles and posted armed
sentries. They confirmed forty-seven-year-old Olson
as commander and made plans to develop an active,

well-armed, and public militia with a presence in all of Michigan's eighty-three counties. They also performed a few paramilitary exercises, practicing maneuvers that would be used if they were forced to defend themselves in battle.

Local officials in Pellston were furious.

"When Reverend Olson called me, I thought he wanted to use the park for a church picnic," said the exasperated mayor, Mary Hessel. "They asked to use the pavilion, but they didn't say they were going to come with guns, with their faces blacked out and in camouflage."

But to Olson, the public display of uniforms and guns was central to the militia's mission.

Olson recalls what he told the troops assembled at the Pellston village park: "I said, 'If we are going to do this right, we are going to have to be proud Americans. Proud enough to wear our uniforms and carry our guns wherever we go, to practice in public and to let the public see who we are.'"

Others had argued that the militia should be a secret underground organization. To go public, they feared, would be to invite government infiltration. But Olson was firm. "We dare not go underground, because then of course we lose our legitimacy. People become suspicious of that which they cannot see."

With painted faces, paramilitary uniforms, big guns, and a dispute with the local government following their first meeting, the Michigan Militia quickly attracted the attention of the bewildered local press. Who were these men and why were they running around dressed like that?

In November 1993 Olson and Southwell first started talking about forming an armed group patterned after the militias that fought the Revolutionary

War. Olson said they were bothered by Waco and by new gun-control laws being passed by Congress. And Southwell, a real-estate agent for ReMax Realty in Petrosky, was especially upset with the state of the public schools attended by his three children. He saw the "Education 2000" school-reform program pushed by Presidents Bush and Clinton as a conspiracy to indoctrinate "socialistic values" into schoolkids across the country.

They saw doom in the future. "I'd guess that within the next two years, you will see the Constitution suspended. . . . Christian fundamentalists will be the first to go under fascism this time. Just like Jews were the first last time."

What Southwell saw coming was a battle of good against evil. "I went to talk to Norm Olson, who is my pastor. I said, 'I'm concerned about what's going on in this country. I see the evil. I'm concerned about my family,'" Southwell said. "Norm Olson and I said we'd help defend each other. I'd go to his house; he'd go to my house. We have to let the tyrants, the politicians, and the bureaucrats know that we are taking a stand. When martial law is declared, I'm gonna have my neighbor there helping me."

As a first step, Olson started a gun shop called the Alanson Armory in Alanson, Michigan, located just a few miles from the church where he served as head pastor. "I'm a pistol-packing preacher because I sell Bibles and guns on the same shelf," Olson said.

Some of the parishioners at Calvary Baptist Church were shocked to see their pastor preaching the Gospel on Sundays and selling deadly weapons every other day of the week. And Olson's sermons were getting more and more fiery. He wasn't afraid to defend his gun shop.

"Our God is not a wimp. He's the God of righteousness and wrath. Our way of looking at God and country is not passive Christianity," he told his parishioners, adding, "In the colonial days, parishioners brought their guns to the chapel."

Norman Olson was ready for battle long before he became a pastor. Immediately after graduating from high school in 1964, he joined the Air Force. He was ready to serve his country; he was ready to go to Vietnam. Despite having just married, he was sent off for two and a half years of duty during the Vietnam War. Stationed first in Guam and then in Thailand, he served in the Tactical Unit Operations Center. With twenty years of military experience, Olson was honorably discharged in 1984 as a master sergeant.

With his three children nearly grown, Olson settled down to a quiet life in the sparsely populated hills of northern Michigan, collecting his Air Force pension and serving as a guest preacher at Calvary Baptist Church in Brutus, Michigan. In 1989 Olson became the head pastor of the church. By the fall of 1993 he was opening a gun shop and talking to Southwell about forming a Colonial-style militia. They started to have small meetings of ten to fifteen people at the church to make plans for their militia. The fact was, Norman Olson missed military life; he was once again ready to go to battle.

Olson had defined the militia as a servant of the local community; he said it would be there to serve the Emmett County sheriff in the event of natural or man-made disasters. So it was ironic that the Michigan Militia's first battle was with the village leaders of Pellston.

After the militia's first meeting, town officials had banned guns in the park. Olson's brigade showed up at the park with their guns for their next meeting, but this time the weapons were unloaded. Not satisfied, Pellston officials revoked the group's permit to assemble in the park.

Olson blasted village officials as "fearful peasants" who were violating the group's Second Amendment right to keep and bear arms. He moved the next militia assembly to a state-owned campground less than a mile from the park. The fifteen-site campground had been operated by the village for decades, and local officials didn't want it turned into a staging area for war games.

"You have this park where people fish in the Maple River and hunt. But having guys there in black-face is scaring people away," said town attorney Wayne Richard Smith. "We won't maintain that campground for the militia, and no one else is going to use it if they're there."

The village extended its firearms ban to the campground, but the Michigan Militia appealed to the state's Department of Natural Resources. The DNR ruled that the militia was not violating state law.

Norm Olson won his first battle without firing a shot.

But the victory was short-lived. The village council responded by voting to suspend operation of the campground. Water spigots were removed, outhouses boarded up, and signs taken down. All Norman Olson's militia had accomplished was to close down a popular campground. He responded by threatening to file federal lawsuits and to create a "citizens' grand jury" to charge officials with violating the Constitution. Eventually he simply moved the militia training exercises to a more remote state park.

The controversy earned Olson and Southwell guest

appearances on local talk radio and attention in the local newspapers. The publicity shocked Southwell's boss at ReMax Realty; Southwell was fired. The ensuing economic hardship rendered him almost destitute. But with his visions of civil war on the horizon, he had more important things to worry about. His troubles only added to his belief that he was a noble patriot fighting a powerful and evil enemy. Like so many others who joined militias, Southwell was ready for martyrdom.

"I have to accept the idea that my life will never be the same," he said. "I sold everything I own and turned my house over to my son. I'm ready to take whatever abuse comes. We are taking a stand and we are prepared to lose everything."

Once the Michigan Militia Corps hit the newspapers, the group began attracting new members from throughout the state. Within six months, the group would have brigades established in sixty-three of Michigan's eighty-three counties and would claim membership of over ten thousand.

Most of the press reports described the Michigan Militia as a wacky and potentially dangerous fringe group, but Olson didn't mind.

"Lie about us or tell the truth. It's still fodder for our cannons," Olson tells reporters. "We love it. We appreciate it. We are going to grow either way. We've helped turn the entire patriot community against the press, against the liberal media, and help them seek other alternative sources of news."

Those alternative news sources helped spread the Michigan Militia's message nationally. Shortly after the group's founding, Southwell journeyed down to Indianapolis to meet with Linda Thompson, who was doing militia organizing of her own. She agreed to distribute the Michigan Militia manual through her computer network.

The manual served as a guidebook for starting a militia. It detailed a chain of command and a code of conduct that included orders on what a militiaman must do if taken as a prisoner of war: "When questioned, should I become a prisoner of war, I am bound to give only name, rank, and date of birth." When Timothy McVeigh was first charged with the bombing of the Oklahoma City federal building, the FBI reported that he responded to questions only by giving his name, rank, and serial number.

The manual also outlined the minimum weapons requirements: "Militia members are required to remain proficient in the maintenance and safe operation of the rifle and to have 100 rounds of ammunition available at all times. The militia member's knapsack shall consist of necessary items to be determined based on the member's assignment. The knapsack, thus outfitted, will be kept available at all times for rapid deployment by the militia member."

Under the direction of member Ken Adams, who owned a marketing company, the group further spread its message by producing videotapes. The tapes were technical instructional guides to equipping militias and preparing for a protracted guerrilla war.

In the video *Equipping the Modern Minuteman*, Mark Price, who is described as a Vietnam veteran and "colonel" in the Michigan Militia, spends over an hour detailing the equipment—including everything from guns and ammo to canteens and bandages—each militiaman needs "for general combat support." Price begins the video by showing a picture of the chopper he flew over Vietnam.

"I spent approximately twenty months in Vietnam,

serving and flying," Price somberly tells the camera. He is wearing a camouflage militia uniform that bears his rank and the insignia of the Michigan Militia. "I spent the entire time in the combat zone. I feel if I went that far away to protect their freedom, which unfortunately failed, I really feel that I need to be involved here to stand for liberty and what is true and just and right." This sentiment is found in militias throughout the country. They have attracted a large number of Vietnam veterans, many of whom believe they were tools of a government conspiracy during the war. If war comes to American soil, they want to be ready to fight and, this time, to win.

While the Michigan Militia expanded as a public, uniformed brigade of citizen soldiers, a group in Noxon, Montana, prepared for revolution in a very different way.

John Trochmann and his family founded the Militia of Montana at about the same time as Olson and Southwell called the first meeting of the Michigan Militia. But the Militia of Montana didn't have uniforms and didn't call for any public training exercises. Located in Noxon, a town surrounded by mountains with a population of 650, the Militia of Montana's headquarters served as an information clearinghouse for militia information, conspiracy theories, and warnings of doom.

From their information command post in Noxon, the Militia of Montana distributed start-up kits for people around the country who wanted to start their own militias. The Noxon office was to be public, open even to the press, but for the actual gun-toting militia, the Militia of Montana suggested a more secretive approach. Militias, the group's manual instructed, should be formed in a seven-man "cell structure."

Unlike the public brigades of the Michigan Militia, these cells would be secretive underground operations. This approach, according to the manual, "will allow security from infiltration and subterfuge." The manual explained, "When one of the members of your cell recruits a new member, bringing your number to eight, three of your eight will break off to form a new cell. The other four, which includes the leader, will stay behind in the old cell. Both of these cells will now grow to seven again." The goal is eventually to have a nationwide network of these mini-militias, or cells, all essentially independent but working for the same goals. "If one cell messes up," the manual says, "the network as a whole will not fail."

Advocates of the public militia didn't like the underground approach.

"When John Trochmann showed me his diagram of cell organization, I said, 'That's the organization of a terrorist group. That's the way the Irish Republican Army is organized. The militia must be public and it must be organized into brigades and battalions,'" said Sam Sherwood, the founder of the United States Militia Association in Blackfoot, Idaho.

The cell structure seems to take a page out of the book of an American terrorist group: the Ku Klux Klan. In the book *Leaderless Resistance*, KKK leader Louis Beam spells out the secret to waging a successful war of racial hatred: "Utilizing the Leaderless Resistance concept, all individuals and groups operate independently of each other, and never report to a central headquarters or single leader for direction or instruction. . . . Participants in a program of Leaderless Resistance through Phantom Cell or individual action must know exactly what they are doing."

"Organs of information distribution," Beam wrote, "such as newspapers, leaflets, computers, etc., which are widely available to all, keep each person informed of events, allowing for a planned response that will take many variations. No one need issue an order to anyone."

The Militia of Montana, or M.O.M., as the group calls itself, started out quietly in January 1994 with less fanfare than its counterparts in other states. By April, however, when the movement started heating up, the group had become one of the most influential militia organizations in the country. Its aggressive distribution of militia start-up kits earned it the nickname "Mother of All Militias."

A fact-finding report by the Anti-Defamation League, an antiracist watchdog, reported, "The Militia of Montana is among the most visible and the most extreme of such groups in the country."

A grandfatherly figure with a thick whitish beard, thin gray eyebrows, and small, piercing dark eyes, John Trochmann looks more like a wise old prophet than a paramilitary leader. He doesn't dress in military fatigues. Cowboy boots, jeans, and button-down shirts are fine by him. He's a full-time revolutionary who doesn't need a uniform. His militia is a family operation. He runs it with his wife, Carolyn, his brother David, and his nephew Randy.

M.O.M. headquarters is located on a dirt road on the edge of Noxon. A no-frills green building made of sheet metal and concrete, it has five small, cluttered rooms and a root cellar out back. The town itself is surrounded by virtually impassable snow-covered mountains and ravines full of elk, bighorn sheep, black bears, and even a few mountain lions. The only way to get to Noxon by car is over a one-lane bridge that crosses the Clark Fork River. This is the Militia of Montana's fortress—its command central.

John Trochmann moved to this serene mountain setting from his native Minnesota in 1988, a year after marrying Carolyn, a Montana native. "One of the qualifications for us marrying each other was that she learned how to downhill-ski and I learned how to square-dance, which we both did," he said. But more important than square dancing and skiing was a shared obsession with guns and conspiracy theories.

"My mom taught me how to shoot, and my dad taught me how to cook," Carolyn, a fifty-one-year-old mother of three, says. Her first two firearms were rifles, a .22 caliber and the much more powerful 30.06 caliber. Now she carries a small pistol with her at all times. "If some bastard comes through that door with ill intent for me, I'll drop him at the door."

John Trochmann has been worrying about conspiracy theories since he was in elementary school. "When I was nine years old, my dad pulled us out of the Lutheran Church because it was joining the World Council of Churches. He said that was one-world government, and he didn't want to be a part of it. In the late 1950s, he also pulled out of the evangelical churches because they were doing the same thing. From that point on, I was very questioning as to what this is all about and what was going on."

In 1960, seventeen-year-old John Trochmann dropped out of high school and joined the Navy. He was sent to Cuba during the missile crisis of 1962, when the Soviet Union and the United States came to the brink of war over Soviet nuclear missiles being placed in Cuba. The crisis ended when the Soviets agreed to remove the missiles. That, Trochmann says, was when he caught his first glimpse of the conspiratorial forces that control the federal government.

"One of the missions we had in Cuba was to take pictures of the Soviet ships taking the missiles back out of Cuba. The pictures that we took I do not believe were of missiles; I believe they were barrels lying end-to-end covered in tarps. I don't think the missiles ever left, which really made me question what was going on with our country," Trochmann explained grimly.

Next came the assassination of President John F. Kennedy. Trochmann watched it on television from a military base in Norfolk, Virginia. He was certain the assassination was the work of the Secret Service, which he insists shot President Kennedy from inside the car that carried him. Why they would kill the man they were sworn to protect, he did not know. But he was certain they did it. "Why? That's my question. Why? Just leave it at that."

In February 1965 Trochmann was honorably discharged from the Navy. He moved back to Minnesota, where he worked as a mechanic in an automobile repair shop. In 1972 he and his brothers David and Dick started their own business in the town of Delano, Troch's Sno-Stuff, which manufactured and distributed snowmobile parts. At the height of the business's success, Trochmann said, he had sixty employees and five thousand wholesale clients, but by the early 1980s business started to fade. Trochmann blamed it on federal regulations.

"We sold it because the tail started wagging the dog. If it wasn't OSHA, it was EPA. If it wasn't EPA, it was IRS. We just got fed up with government intervention everywhere we went. Government intervention destroyed our business; we sold it while it was still worth something."

The business's troubles may have been John Trochmann's own doing. Over the objections of his brother Dick, he started sending out extremist political literature with the company's monthly mailing, like a trial run for the mailings of the Militia of Montana.

"We sent out bits and pieces of literature explaining the erosion of our country, the insurgency of the one-world takeover of each nation of the earth. One of them was called 'Billions for the Bankers, Debts for the People.' It showed the three types of slavery on earth. And the sneakiest way to do it is through finances, and that's how we felt America was going to be enslaved."

John and David sold their last pieces of the business in 1984, leaving part of it with their brother Dick. David moved out to Montana, to be followed by John four years later.

John says he got involved in "community affairs" once he moved to Montana: "Meetings with commissioners, community food bank programs, various things to help the community." But in 1989, he sent his three children off to a "family day" retreat at the headquarters of the Aryan Nations, a virulently racist neo-Nazi hate group.

When he went to pick up his kids, Trochmann said he was appalled. But not by the group's racism, not by the *Whites Only* signs that mark its property, and not by its near worship of Adolf Hitler. In the words of his wife, Carolyn: "My children had been up all night, and there had been no supervision or discipline. There was lots of alcohol, and one woman there was very promiscuous. So I spoke my mind and made a decision never to go back there again."

But John Trochmann did return—as a featured speaker at the 1990 World Congress of the Aryan Nations. He insists he never joined the Aryan Nations and that he used his speech to scold them for their "immorality," which he described as the alcohol abuse and promiscuity—not racism and Hitler worship.

Richard Butler, the leader of the Aryan Nations, said of the speech, "He rambled on about something, didn't make much of an impression on me. Though he seemed to agree with our goals at that time. At least, that's what he told me."

Trochmann now angrily denies that he is racist or anti-Semitic. "The militia doesn't exclude anyone," he says.

Samuel Sherwood, the head of the United States Militia Association in Idaho, says that he has heard Trochmann express the racist, anti-Semitic views of the Christian Identity movement. Christian Identity defines Jews as the descendants of Satan and Aryans as God's only chosen people. Trochmann has now backed away from those views, Sherwood says, for tactical reasons: "They found out that the press is going to pick on them and people aren't going to join them and buy their books and videotapes and everything. So they've cooled it on the religious fervor side and upped the heat on the political diatribe side."

Trochmann had been trying to get a political movement going ever since his onetime friend Randy Weaver had his deadly showdown with federal authorities in August 1992. With the militia movement he found a way to attract a wider audience for his conspiracy theories; he just needed to, in his words, "leave religion at the door."

Sometimes he slips. In a January 1995 interview with *Esquire* magazine reporter Daniel Voll, he said of the militia movement, "Blacks, Jews are welcome. But when America is the new Israel, they'll need to go back where they came from. It's just nature's law— kind should go unto kind."[1]

As hollow as Trochmann's denials sound, the Militia of Montana was not preaching race war; it was preaching the militia's view of the Constitution. So were the militias forming in Texas, Michigan, and other states around the country. The momentum was building.

---

[1] Voll's account of the interview is in the March 1995 issue of *Esquire,* page 48.

Liberal academics view the Second Amendment as an embarrassment, like the drunken uncle who shows up at the family reunion. They would never be so cavalier with an amendment they like.

—*Sanford Levinson in the Yale Law Review*

Somebody's blood on down the street might run, If they ever try to come and take my gun.

—*Patriot folk-rocker Carl Klang in "Leave Our Guns Alone"*

"A document secretly delivered to me reveals frightening evidence that the full-scale war to crush your gun rights has not only begun, but is well underway," wrote Wayne R. LaPierre, Jr., in the June 1994 issue of *American Rifleman,* the magazine of the National Rifle Association (NRA). His "special report" was titled "The Final War Has Begun."

The warning wasn't coming from a fringe lunatic; LaPierre is the executive vice president of the NRA, an organization with 3.5 million members and enough political muscle to make it one of the most powerful lobbying groups in America.

"What's more," LaPierre's special report continued, "dozens of Federal gun ban bills suggest this final assault has begun—not just to ban all handguns or all semi-automatics, but to eliminate private firearms ownership completely and forever. I firmly believe the NRA has no alternative but to recognize this attack and counter with every resource we can *muster*." [Emphasis added.]

Thousands of Americans on the radical end of the gun-rights movement were ready to take LaPierre's words seriously—and literally. In the *Random House College Dictionary,* the first definition of muster is:

> **mus•ter (mus´tər),** *v.t.* **1.** to assemble
> (troops, a ship's crew, etc.), as for battle
> or inspection.

Nothing fuels the militia movement more than fear of a systematic attempt by the government to take away citizens' guns, or, as the feared plan is often called, "a great gun grab." After all, the Weaver and Waco incidents both began with federal authorities attempting to enforce federal gun laws. Congressman Steve Stockman, a Texas Republican supportive of the militia movement, summed up the way thousands of gun-rights advocates viewed the Waco firestorm: "These men, women, and children were burned to death because they owned guns that the government did not want them to have."[1]

Many gun-rights activists viewed the armed federal agents storming the Branch Davidian compound as a

---

[1] Stockman's comments are from an article he wrote in the June 1995 issue of *Guns and Ammo.* He also wrote: "Had Bill Clinton really been unhappy with what Attorney General Janet Reno ordered, he would not only have fired her, he would have had Reno indicted for premeditated murder."

horrible vision of the future, when federal agents would go from house to house to confiscate guns.

Not long after the Waco incident, Congress passed a landmark gun-control law, the Brady bill. The Brady bill, which mandates a five-day waiting period for all handgun purchases, is named after James Brady, a former press secretary for President Ronald Reagan. Brady was shot in the head and paralyzed during the assassination attempt on President Reagan in 1981. The shooter, John Hinckley, Jr., used a handgun. After the incident, James Brady and his wife, Sarah, became two of America's foremost advocates of gun control. Lobbying from his wheelchair, his speech impaired by Hinckley's bullet, Brady fought for the bill for more than a decade; when it passed, gun-rights advocates warned that the Great Gun Grab was under way.

Ken Toole of the Montana Human Rights Network describes the effect the Brady bill had in the West: "With the Brady bill it was like someone poured jet fuel on the movement. Overnight, we saw all this militia stuff bleed right out of the white supremacists, who had been pushing the idea for years, and engulf entire communities."

The NRA had "mustered" all its political resources to fight the Brady bill, but it lost. Radical gun-rights advocates felt they had to try something new. They turned to the Second Amendment of the U.S. Constitution: "A well regulated Militia, being necessary to the security of a free State, the right of the people to keep and bear Arms shall not be infringed."

Gun-rights advocates have always pointed to the Second Amendment as evidence that gun control is unconstitutional. But they usually pointed to the

second part of the amendment, "the right of the people to keep and bear Arms shall not be infringed."
Almost always ignored was the reference to "a well
regulated Militia."

But what exactly is a militia? The *Random House
College Dictionary* defines it this way:

> **mi•li•tia (mi li´sh ə)**, *n.* **1.** a body of men
> enrolled for military service, and called out
> periodically for drill and exercise but serv-
> ing full time only in emergencies. **2.** *(U.S.)*
> all able-bodied males of each state
> between 18 and 45 years of age considered
> eligible for military service. **3.** a body of
> citizen soldiers as distinguished from pro-
> fessional soldiers.

In colonial America, the militia was simply adult
citizens who would be ready to grab their muskets
and fight in the event of an emergency. The colonies
didn't have standing armies; defense was left to citizen soldiers. In times of peace, able-bodied adults
were simply considered an unorganized militia. The
colonial governments had the power to call up, or
muster, this unorganized militia when needed.

The Constitution, in Article One, Section 8, gives
the government the power to "provide for calling
forth the militia." Section 8 further says, "Congress
shall have power . . . to provide for organizing, arming, and disciplining, the militia, and for governing
such part of them as may be employed in the service
of the United States."

Legal experts differ widely on the meaning of the
Second Amendment. As *Time* magazine put it, "The
Second Amendment is like a Rorschach test:

observers tend to examine it and discover whatever they already believe about gun control."

For Harvard law professor Lawrence Tribe, the mention of militias puts a limit on the Second Amendment guarantee of the right to own guns. "The Second Amendment's preamble makes it clear that it is not designed to create an individual right to bear arms outside the context of a state-run militia," he says. For Tribe, as well as for many other legal experts, the well-regulated militia in the Second Amendment refers to government-run entities such as the National Guard.

The Supreme Court has generally agreed with Professor Tribe; no federal gun-control laws have ever been struck down on Second Amendment grounds.

But the founders of the militia movement and many other gun-rights advocates see the Second Amendment in absolute terms. Its purpose, they believe, is to give individuals the power—through the right to own firearms—to fight off a tyrannical government. Government, they reason, is less likely to take away rights when the citizens are armed. Here they tap into an old American tradition that comes right out of the Declaration of Independence, which asserted the right of the people to "alter or abolish" an unjust government. Without their armed militia, the colonists would have been unable to "abolish" King George's rule over his American colonies.

"I believe that the Second Amendment is the guarantor of the others. You cannot name one dictatorship that didn't start by disarming the people," explains Brad Alpert, a member of the 51st Militia in Missouri.

Like many militia members, Alpert takes his cue from a radical gun-rights group called Jews for the

Preservation of Firearms Ownership (JPFO). Founded
in 1989 by Milwaukee gun dealer and Vietnam veteran Aaron Zelman, JPFO is a staunch foe of gun control and a frequent defender of the militia movement.
The group distributes a poster of Adolf Hitler giving
his one-armed salute. Underneath the picture of
Hitler, the caption reads: "All in favor of gun control
raise your right hand." They argue that Hitler began
his path to dictatorship and mass murder with gun
control. If the Jews in Germany had been armed, JPFO
reasons, there would have been no Holocaust. JPFO
also argues that every other murderous dictator of the
twentieth century—including Pol Pot in Cambodia,
Stalin in the Soviet Union, and Mao in China—consol-
idated their power through gun control.

Ohio militia leader James Johnson, who is black,
extends the theory to slavery in the United States.
Speaking in front of the Lincoln Memorial in
Washington, D.C., in May 1995, Johnson told a gun-
rights rally, "For any black person out there listening,
take this message and burn it in your brain: If our ances-
tors had been armed, they would not have been slaves."

For militia members, gun-control laws in the
United States—such as the Brady bill—are not merely
a violation of the Second Amendment. They are a
step toward dictatorship in America, or, as the title of
a JPFO book says, *Gun Control: Gateway to Tyranny*.
JPFO insists that the 1968 U.S. Gun Control Act,
which gave the federal government power to regulate
the sale of firearms, is directly patterned after a 1938
law from Nazi Germany. They call the act "Hitler's
last legacy."

In 1994, as militias were forming across the country,
Congress passed yet another gun-control law. The
1994 crime bill included a ban on the manufacture of

nineteen kinds of assault weapons. It was another political defeat for the NRA, but it drove more gun-rights activists into militias. The bill, however, did not ban the sale or ownership of the weapons.

"The main motivating factor for this recent upsurge in activity," Texas militiaman Jon Roland said in April 1994, "has been the ill-conceived gun-control provisions of the current crime bill. People everywhere see it not only as a major assault on their constitutional rights to keep and bear arms, but as a more sinister preparation for depriving them of their other constitutional rights after they have been disarmed. They perceive a greater threat from criminal officials than from criminal street gangs."

With the passing of the second federal gun-control law in two years—compounded by the deadly effort to enforce gun laws in Waco—militia members saw tyranny on the horizon. Government was taking away guns; what would be next?

Congressman Steve Stockman again expressed the feelings of the rank-and-file militia members: "The assault-weapon ban had the advantage of making certain that a potentially tyrannical government would have less to fear from an aroused and angry citizenry."

Following the passage of the assault-weapon ban, talk-show host G. Gordon Liddy spread the message over the airwaves, warning that the Great Gun Grab was part of a master scheme to accomplish something far more sinister. "The gun owners of this country used to say, 'They're coming for your guns,' and that was certainly true enough and it is certainly still true. But unfortunately what we have to say now, to all Americans, is they are coming for your rights, virtually all of them."

Liddy said it was time for civil disobedience. "Now the Constitution is absolutely crystal clear. Any law which infringes upon your right to keep and bear arms—any arms of your choice—is unconstitutional. Just don't obey the damn law."

As the Brady bill and the assault-weapon ban became law in 1993 and 1994, something else was happening. Across America, people were stockpiling weapons. In 1993 and 1994 firearms sales reached record numbers. During this two-year period, more than ten million new handguns, shotguns, and rifles were sold in the United States—an increase of more than three million over the number of new firearms sold during the previous two years.[2] The militia was well armed.

---

[2] Russ Thurman, "Shooting Industries Firearm Business Analysis," *Shooting Industry*, 1995, pp. 98–101.

BLACK HELICOPTERS ON THE HORIZON

6

Most assuredly, terror will reign.

—*Mark Koernke,*
America in Peril

"They got it all wrong. Mark took the rap for the four other guys with him. That's just the kind of guy he is."

John Stadtmiller was objecting to *Time* magazine's version of an incident that occurred more than twenty years ago involving his friend and partner, Mark Koernke.

The way *Time* told the story, the young Koernke was a loner with exotic ideas and a fascination with secret places. To illustrate the point, *Time* described how his high-school history teacher heard noises coming from under the classroom floorboards during one of his lectures.

"I walked over, and there was a trap door in the floor that led into some maintenance tunnels for access to the heating pipes," the teacher, Hank

Flandysz, told *Time*. "The trapdoor lifted up, and there looking up at me was Mark Koernke."

It's a true story, but Stadtmiller says Mark wasn't acting alone. He was exploring secret passageways at Dexter High School with four other guys; when he made the wrong turn into Flandysz's classroom, he signaled the others to make a quiet getaway. Koernke was the only one to get in trouble for snooping around the school's maintenance tunnels.

In Stadtmiller's version of the story, Mark Koernke stood up and paid the price for his actions so that the others could get away free: "That's just the kind of guy he is."

Why America's preeminent newsmagazine would care about what Mark Koernke did as a teenager in Dexter, Michigan, is another story. *Time* dedicated six full pages of its June 21, 1995, issue to the life story of Koernke, a maintenance worker at the University of Michigan. A janitor.

But Koernke is no ordinary maintenance worker. In fact, there's nothing ordinary about him at all.

He is perhaps the single most influential figure in the militia movement. "Mark from Michigan," as he is known to fellow revolutionaries, has given speeches in forty-four states and produced three videotapes that have reached hundreds of thousands, perhaps more than a million, patriots across the country. He was one of the first to aggressively encourage the formation of citizens' militias and, at a speech organized by Norm Olson in February 1994, inspired the founding of the Michigan Militia. The daily radio program he cohosts with Stadtmiller, *The Intelligence Report*, hit shortwave radio in August 1994, extending his influence to all fifty states. Listeners transcribe his broadcasts and distribute them to thousands more through fax networks, computer networks, and the Internet.

Koernke served as an army reservist with the 70th Division in Livonia, Michigan, from 1977 to 1983. During that time he also attended army intelligence school in Fort Huachuca in Arizona, achieving the rank of E–5 specialist, the equivalent of a sergeant. He spent no time on active duty analyzing intelligence, but his army records show that he qualified as a sharpshooter and hand-grenade expert.

Koernke's first video, *America in Peril,* provided the dark, ominous visions that would haunt the militia movement and encourage its expansion. Produced in the fall of 1993, *America in Peril* outlines the conspiracy theory that in one form or another animates much of the militia movement.

The vision runs like this: Elements within the U.S. government are working with foreign leaders to turn the United States into a dictatorship under the leadership of the United Nations. The battle to create this U.N. dictatorship, known as the new world order, is already well under way. Foreign troops are already training on American soil for a planned attack on Americans who resist; a network of forty-three detention centers has been set up throughout the country to serve as concentration camps for the resisters; plans have been readied to control the population through microchips to be implanted in newborn babies and through radio boxes already in place in automobiles made after 1985.

It sounds crazy. It is crazy. But Koernke musters thousands of pages of government documents, eyewitness reports, and other evidence that he insists prove that the nefarious plan is already in motion. And thousands of people in the militia movement believe him and have stocked up on weapons, ammunition, and food to prepare for the war Koernke predicts is coming soon. Others don't believe everything he says but certainly think he's on to something.

In *America in Peril*, Koernke stands at a podium in a room that is empty except for a couple of people manning the video cameras. He wears a dark gray suit, a gray tie, and thick glasses. He talks on and on for an hour and fifty-two minutes, outlining what he calls "the new world order operations in the United States." Although his delivery is a bit dull and occasionally monotone, he speaks with the conviction and seriousness of someone who senses that his enemy is closing in, that his life is in danger. If he's going to die at the hands of the forces of the new world order, he doesn't want his message to die with him. So he goes into an empty room and speaks for nearly two hours in front of a video camera. Now the forces of the new world order can't stop his message by simply stopping him.

"The printed word is going to be banned. Take my word for it. I guarantee it," he tells the camera.

The battle against the forces he describes will not be easy, but Koernke makes it clear he's not afraid to be a martyr: "Can we win? Absolutely. Will we win? It will be a long, drawn-out, rotten, nasty affair I would prefer not to see at all. But if we have a choice between freedom and slavery, I would rather gladly die standing on my feet with a weapon in my hand than die in a ditch on my knees, begging that somebody not put a bullet in the back of my head."

As his friend John Stadtmiller would say, that's just the kind of guy he is.

In Koernke's vision, the new world order's strategy begins, not surprisingly, with gun control. In most of the conspiracy theories whirling through the militia movement, the enemy begins with the Great Gun Grab.

"Now, it should be noted," Koernke tells the video camera, "before they perform any of the actions that are pending, they are going to have to take the weapons that we have in the United States."

Koernke says the gun grab—which will be accomplished by house-to-house searches and seizures of all weapons—will be carried out by a secret government entity he calls the "multi-jurisdictional task force police," or MJTF. Unknown to just about anybody but Koernke, the MJTF is made up of military personnel, state and local law enforcement, and street gangs.

"Both the Crips and the Bloods [two notorious Los Angeles street gangs] are being trained, equipped, and uniformed with federal funding through California," he says, explaining that street gangs will be the "cannon fodder" of the new world order. They'll be the first ones sent in to grab citizens' guns. "Their mission is to be the forefront of the master forces to come through the door. . . . They're thugs, but they're expendable thugs. Remember that." In this view, the L.A. riots of 1992 were simply a trial run for what is to come.

"Most assuredly," he says, "terror shall reign."

Once the populace is disarmed, the new world order can solidify its domination of the United States and the rest of the world. The states will be dissolved and America divided into ten regions with governors appointed by the president. There will be no more elections. The United States will simply become a part of the United Nations, or, as he tells the video camera, "a small corporate entity, part of a larger company."

Foreign troops, under U.N. command, figure
prominently in the plan. They are organized under
what Koernke calls the Financial Crimes Enforcement
Network (FINCEN). He compares the FINCEN
troops to the Hessian mercenaries hired by the British
to fight American colonists. They are highly trained,
well paid, and ruthless. On the video, Koernke says
two brigades of professional mercenary forces made
up of Nepalese Gurkhas are already on American
soil—in northern Montana, to be exact—training for
a war against American citizens.

Another major player in the new world order's
plan, Koernke says, is the Federal Emergency
Management Administration (FEMA). FEMA seems
like a benign federal agency; its stated mission is to
provide emergency relief to regions struck by natural
disaster. Its employees are dispatched to provide shel-
ter, food, and other resources following major floods,
hurricanes, earthquakes and disasters.

But Koernke says FEMA's main mission has nothing to do with disaster relief. FEMA's primary goal,
according to Koernke and many other militia leaders,
is to lay the groundwork for the new world order by
setting up detention camps that will hold prisoners of
war and other gun-owning Americans who resist the
new world order's attempt to take over America. He
claims to have located forty-three such camps already
under construction in the United States.

"FEMA is not Federal Emergency Management
Agency. FEMA is the secret government, legally,"
Koernke says. "FEMA has approximately three thousand six hundred employees, and yet of the three thousand six hundred employees, only about fifty-nine to
sixty-three actually deal with emergency management
such as storms, disasters, hurricanes, or man-made

catastrophes. If only sixty of them are doing this, let me ask you one very basic question: What are the other three thousand six hundred doing?"

To view the attack force of the new world order, Koernke says, "observe the air, not the ground." There you will see FINCEN's "rotary-wing aircraft assets"—black helicopters.

Black helicopters are the nightmare vision of the militia movement. Koernke is far from the only one to talk about them. Black-helicopter sightings are continually reported on shortwave radio and throughout the underground network of patriot media. Linda Thompson claims black helicopters regularly spy on her and have even shot at her. In *America in Peril*, Koernke explains the origin of the notorious black helicopters:

> Back in the early part of 1990, approximately three thousand rotary-wing aircraft were withdrawn from our strategic reserve. These are not from our Reserve or Guard; these came from the mothball fleet. Upon implementing this force, these units were transferred to FINCEN and painted in flat black, not flat green and not camouflage green.
>
> These aircraft are in flat black. They bear no markings or identification to determine whether they are American or foreign national. And the fact of the matter is they are now foreign national assets, no longer in the hands of the United States Air Force. We do supply and support them with your tax dollars . . . but we do not control them completely now.

Militia members are part of a grass-roots movement without a national leadership and are extremely
distrustful of any authority, even militia leaders. In
this context, Mark Koernke has helped to mold opinion among militia activists, but his word is not the
last. His "intelligence gathering" is extremely influential, but others do similar work and reach slightly different conclusions. The conspiracy theories all see
dictatorship on the horizon, but they each have their
own style and add their own unique research as they
put the pieces together.

The Militia of Montana (M.O.M.), for instance,
also sees FEMA preparing concentration camps, but
they say the U.S. will be divided into nine regions,
not the ten regions predicted by Koernke. M.O.M.
also adds another element to the conspiracy: weather
warfare. M.O.M. says they have documents proving
that elements within the United Nations and the federal government have developed a way to use
weather against U.S. citizens. This new technology
can create natural disasters—including tornadoes,
floods, blizzards, and hurricanes—on demand.
Weather warfare will be one of the tools used by the
United Nations, M.O.M. literature says, to wipe out
half the world's population by the year 2000. "We've
got the documents to prove it," says M.O.M. leader
John Trochmann.

Texas militia leader Jon Roland borrows his conspiracy from a notion common among left-wing conspiracy theorists: that a shadow government made up
of politicians, CIA operatives, and business leaders
has already taken control of much of the U.S. government. "It is sad," Roland said when he started the
Texas Constitutional Militia, "that we now live in a
police state and not in a constitutional republic. If we

are going to solve our common problems, it is going to take all of us working together. Members of the shadow government can't survive unless they return to constitutional governance."

Ray Southwell and Norman Olson of the Michigan Militia reject some of the wilder assertions of Mark Koernke and see most of the conspiracies emanating out of the Central Intelligence Agency.

Like Koernke, Indiana militia leader Linda Thompson predicts a United Nations invasion of the United States. She adds that the troops will be guided by secret symbols that have been placed on the back of highway signs throughout the country. In an April 1994 communiqué to fellow militia members, Thompson wrote, "Troop movement markers (bright colored reflective stickers on the backs of road signs) are already in place in this country, prepared to engage in 'peace keeping' against us." Her theories, complete with video "evidence," are explained in a video entitled *America Under Siege*, which she made a year after Koernke's *America in Peril*.

The conspiracy theories received a boost when Koernke, the Militia of Montana, and others discovered that active-duty marines were given a survey to gauge their opinions on such controversial issues as shooting at civilians and working under U.N. command. Rumors spread that the survey was part of a plan to have U.S. soldiers swear allegiance to the United Nations and begin the much-feared Great Gun Grab.

The militia intelligence-gathering networks were right on this one. The survey was real. It was given on May 10, 1994, to three hundred combat-trained soldiers, all at the Marine Corps Air-Ground Combat Center in California.

But the survey wasn't part of a conspiracy to kill gun owners or turn U.S. forces over to the United Nations. It was conducted by Navy Lt. Commander Guy Cunningham, a master's-degree student at the Naval Postgraduate School in Monterey, California. The survey was for Cunningham's master's thesis, entitled "Peacekeeping and U.N. Operational Control: A Study of Their Effect on Unit Cohesion." Far from a new world order conspirator, Cunningham is highly *critical* of putting any U.S. troops under U.N. command, even for modest peacekeeping missions.

The panic in the militia movement caused by the survey, and the rumors surrounding it, are symptomatic of many militia conspiracy theories: They are based on an element of truth and then wildly overblown into a grand conspiracy.

But the results of Cunningham's survey will give little solace to frightened militia members. Of the three hundred marines surveyed, 26.3 percent said they would fire on U.S. citizens if so ordered; 23.7 percent said they were willing to swear allegiance to the United Nations.

A common thread that runs through almost all of the militia conspiracy theories is the new world order as the ultimate enemy. The phrase "new world order" became common currency in the United States in early 1991. The man who popularized the term wasn't Mark Koernke or some crazed conspiracy theorist.

It was President George Bush.

In several speeches before the Persian Gulf war, President Bush said the world was entering a new era of global cooperation. The old order had been characterized by war and confrontation between two great superpowers, the United States and the Soviet Union.

But the Berlin Wall was now torn down and democracy was on the march through the old Soviet empire. With the Cold War over, Bush predicted "a new world order" based on "a partnership of nations" brokered in part through the United Nations. The first test of Bush's new world order was the Persian Gulf war, or, as the mission was called, Operation Desert Storm. He won a vote of the U.N. Security Council to authorize the war and declared it to be a battle of the world, organized through the United Nations, against Iraqi dictator Saddam Hussein. More than forty nations sent troops and military equipment to participate in the fighting.

On September 11, 1991, with a hundred thousand American troops assembled on the Iraqi border, Bush addressed a special joint session of Congress. He outlined his vision of a "new world order" for the first time:

> A new partnership of nations has begun.
>
> We stand today at a unique and extraordinary moment. The crisis in the Persian Gulf, as grave as it is, also offers a rare opportunity to move toward an historic period of cooperation. Out of these troubled times, our fifth objective—a new world order—can emerge: a new era—freer from the threat of terror, stronger in the pursuit of justice, and more secure in the quest for peace. . . .
>
> Today that new world is struggling to be born. A world quite different from the one we've known. A world where the rule of law supplants the rule of the jungle. A world in which nations recognize the

shared responsibility for freedom and justice. A world where the strong respect the
rights of the weak.

For decades, ultra-right-wing conspiracy theorists,
most notably the John Birch Society, had seen the
United Nations at the center of a conspiracy to bring
about the global domination by Communism. With
Bush's speeches on the new world order and the reality of a U.N.-sanctioned war in the Persian Gulf, a
new generation of conspiracy theorists saw the threat
as even more imminent. In *America in Peril,* Mark
Koernke explains the significance of the gulf war.

"The primary mission of Operation Desert Dust, or
what we call Desert Storm," Koernke says, "was to
see if the American people would eat the new world
order."

Koernke paints an ominous picture of brutality
under the new world order. In *America in Peril,* he
urges everyone to join militias: "Men, women, young,
old. And do not discriminate." The militias, he said,
should be organized "from below" into ten-person
squads made up of friends and neighbors.

If the militia wins, Koernke says, America will be
the constitutional republic envisioned by Thomas
Jefferson, George Washington, and the rest of the
founding fathers. But Koernke's vision of an
American republic, as presented in *America in Peril,*
includes a great purge of nonbelievers that is completely alien to the concepts of individual rights and
representative government put forth by America's
founders. Koernke says:

There are many people in this country who
will not listen to what we are talking about

here. I'm not worried about them. These people are like the population that existed in the United States in 1775. Do not be concerned for them. They'll tag along, or we'll have to ship them overseas when the time comes. I can think of many glorious socialist regimes who would be more than happy to take in a few more slaves.

I don't say that we hang them or shoot them. There's a lot of people who'd like to do that. I think the best punishment is to brand their butts, give them one piece of luggage, and ship their hind end overseas, where they can live out the rest of their lives outside this constitutional republic and see how we flourish from afar.

Koernke's contempt for the mainstream of American society, exhibited clearly in this excerpt from *America in Peril,* is not unusual in the militia movement, where the masses are often referred to as "sheeple" mindlessly obeying a corrupt federal government. And it did not slow the growth of the movement. As the visions of black helicopters on the horizon spread across America, more and more people were ready for the big battle to come.

The tree of liberty must be refreshed from time to time with the blood of patriots and tyrants.

—Thomas Jefferson,
November 13, 1787

DIGGING IN 7

"ALERT!!

"ALL MILITIA UNITS WILL CONVENE at 8:00 A.M., Monday, September 19, 1994, in Washington, D.C., armed and in uniform, to deliver the Declaration of Independence to the White House and to enforce the ultimatum. The militia will arrest Congressmen who have failed to uphold their oaths of office, who then will be tried for Treason by Citizens' courts."

It was April 1994. Militias were forming in more than a dozen states across the country. Linda Thompson decided it was time to take action.

Thompson's call for an armed march on Washington hit the network of alternative "patriot media," and throughout the summer of 1994 it reached thousands of militia organizers across the country. The call to arms was distributed through computer bulletin board services, newsgroups on the Internet, and informal fax networks. It was talked about on shortwave radio and written up in underground newsletters.

The forty-two-year-old Indianapolis lawyer had helped inspire the militia movement with her videotapes of the federal siege of the Branch Davidians in Waco. Now she hoped to lead the troops into battle.

Thompson's alert closed with these words: "Find the local militia in your area. If there is not one, start one. Be in Washington, D.C., in September. Your liberty, your children's future, and this nation's freedom depend on it. Proceed as planned, plan accordingly, and God bless us all."

She signed the document "Linda Thompson, Acting Adjutant General, Unorganized Militia of the United States of America, Pursuant to 10 U.S.C. § 311 and the Constitution of the United States, Articles I and II, Bill of Rights."

As a footnote, she added: "NOTE: MILITIA MEMBERS MUST WEAR IDENTIFYING INSIGNIA AND BE ARMED. If you are armed and wear a military insignia identifying you as a member of a military unit, if captured, you must be treated as a Prisoner of War, not as a criminal arrestee, by law."

A week before Thompson sent out her call to militia members, she sent out an "Ultimatum" and a "Declaration of Independence of 1994" to each and every member of the U.S. Senate and House of Representatives. She added punch to her mailing by sending the documents through certified mail. She wanted to make one thing clear: Linda Thompson and her unorganized militia meant business. The ultimatum was dated April 19, 1994—the one-year anniversary of

In 1992, the federal law enforcement officers closed in on Randy Weaver's tiny plywood cabin in Ruby Ridge, Idaho. In the ensuing twelve-day standoff, a federal marshal and Weaver's wife and son were killed. Weaver was tried for murder, among other charges, but he was acquitted of all of the most serious charges brought against him. In August 1995, Weaver and his family won a $3.1 million settlement from the federal government. Weaver has become a hero and martyr of the militia movement.

Michigan Militia co-founder Ray Southwell addresses the press shortly after the bombing of the federal building in Oklahoma City.

Luiz C. Ribeiro/New York *Post*

Equipped with survival gear, ammunition, and weapons, Captain Blake Whitten participates in a training retreat at a Michigan Militia camp in Wolverine.

Luiz C. Ribeiro/New York *Post*

With high-powered scopes on their rifles, members of the Michigan Militia discuss their training plan at the militia camp in Wolverine, Michigan.

Luiz C. Ribeiro/New York *Post*

The self-styled patriots of the Michigan Militia say they are the true defenders of the American tradition. Here members of the 14th Brigade salute the flag at a training exercise.

© Mark Peterson/Saba

Members of the 14th Brigade of the Michigan Militia, representing the southern part of the state, take a break from training exercises in December 1994.

Shortly after the bombing of the federal building in Oklahoma City, ABC News mistakenly reported that the FBI had initiated a manhunt for Mark Koernke in conjunction with the terrorist attack. But the ABC report was wrong. The FBI announced the next day that Koernke was not suspected in connection with the bombing.

Luiz C. Ribeiro/New York *Post*

On June 15, 1995, the militia movement reached another milestone: testifying before the United States Senate. Ohio militia leader James Johnson (left) and Michigan Militiaman Norman Olson (right) sparred with the senators at a raucous hearing full of conspiracy theories and ominous talk of corruption and civil war. "It's good that we are getting these views aired out because 200 years ago the British didn't get the hint until they saw dead redcoats out there," Johnson told the senators.

Reuter/Bettmann

In December 1994, militia leaders faced off against Phil Donahue before a national television audience. Here an exasperated James Johnson of the Ohio Unorganized Militia (left) listens as Donahue (right) and New Mexico militiaman Bob Wright shout at each other.

Francis Specker/New York *Post*

John Trochmann (left), founder of the Militia of Montana, scolded the Washington press corps at a contentious Capital Hill press conference on May 25, 1995. The press conference was called after the Senate postponed a hearing on the militia movement. Montana militiaman Robert Fletcher (center) and Leroy Crenshaw (right) of Massachusetts also sparred with reporters.

AP Photo/Mark Wilson

Texas militia members place a memorial for the Branch Davidians who died during the April 1993 federal raid of their compound near Waco, Texas.

Fort Worth Star-Telegram/Jerry W. Hoefer

the Waco firestorm and the 219th anniversary of the first battle of the Revolutionary War.

April 19, 1994, was also exactly one year before the bombing of the Alfred P. Murrah Federal Building in Oklahoma City.

Thompson's thousand-word ultimatum provided a laundry list of many of the grievances that were driving people into the militia movement—from gun control to the income tax to federal government intrusion into the everyday lives of citizens. Addressed to "Each Member of the United States House of Representatives and United States Senate," the document was written in the turgid legalese of a lawyer filing court papers, but it revealed a shocking list of demands.

Under the words "YOU ARE COMMANDED," Thompson ordered each Congressman to "do all things necessary" to accomplish Thompson's bizarre demands, which included:

- Repeal the Fourteenth Amendment (which includes the equal-protection clause), the Sixteenth Amendment (which established the federal income tax), and the Seventeenth Amendment (which concerns the election of senators and representatives).

- Repeal the Brady bill.

- Repeal the North American Free Trade Agreement.

- Repeal the Drug Interdiction Act.

- Immediately remove any and all foreign troops and military equipment in the United States.

- Declare that the United States is not operating under the authority of the United Nations.

- Abolish the Federal Reserve and return to the gold standard.

- Declare that "the federal government has no jurisdiction to make or enforce criminal laws outside its territories," which Thompson limited to Washington, D.C., and property actually owned by the U.S. government, such as military bases.

- Conduct a "full Congressional inquiry" into the actions of the federal government during the Waco siege.

The ultimatum gave members of Congress until 8:00 A.M. on September 19, 1994, to begin action on each of her demands.

"If you do not personally and publicly attend to these demands," the ultimatum warned, "you will be identified as a Traitor, and you will be brought up on charges for Treason before a Court of the Citizens of this Country."

The ultimatum didn't say how the treasonous members of Congress would be punished, but Thompson cleared up the confusion during a May 3 interview on the Phoenix radio station KFYI. "The penalty for treason is death by hanging," the self-proclaimed acting adjutant general declared. "And we've got some really nice, tall light poles in downtown Washington, D.C."

With her ultimatum mailed to every member of Congress, Thompson went to work organizing her march, getting signatures for her "Declaration of Independence of 1994," and speaking at rallies across the country. Some of her rallies attracted large, standing-room-only crowds; the *Atlanta Constitution* reported that eight hundred people attended a Thompson rally at the Cobb County Civic Auditorium in Marietta, Georgia.

Joseph Ditzhazy, a member of the Michigan Militia, attended one of Thompson's rallies in the spring of 1994 and was shocked at what he witnessed. He later spoke about it on ABC's *PrimeTime Live*.

"Linda Thompson was showing pictures of senior U.S. officials on the wall and people were standing up, screaming, 'Let's kill them, let's murder them, let's hang them, let's lynch them.'"

Ditzhazy says the pictures were of President Clinton, Hillary Rodham Clinton, then–secretary of the Treasury Lloyd Bentsen, and Attorney General Janet Reno.

"She said, 'Let's take guns to Washington, D.C., take U.S. Senators and Congressmen into custody, hold them for trial, and, if necessary, execute them.'"

The unrestrained rage of the crowd frightened Ditzhazy. He faxed a letter to Vice President Al Gore to report the threats made against U.S. officials. The letter describes how Thompson showed a picture of Secretary Bentsen on a large screen and described him as "a foreign agent, a traitor to the Constitution, and someone who, the audience shouted, should be shot or hung." Gore's office referred Ditzhazy's fax to the Secret Service.

But Thompson's work continued. On July 13 she set out to stop a bus carrying supporters of President

Clinton's health plan through Indianapolis. She parked her vehicle in the path of the oncoming bus and refused to move it. The Indianapolis police arrested her for obstructing traffic. At the time of this writing, the charges were still pending.

When she was arrested, she was carrying a .45 caliber handgun and a .22 caliber pistol. In her vehicle, police found an assault rifle with 295 rounds of ammunition.

In the meantime, Thompson's plans for an armed march on Washington were proving to be about as successful as her attempt to block President Clinton's health-care bus. Militia leaders around the country—including Jon Roland in Texas, Norman Olson in Michigan, John Trochmann in Montana, and Samuel Sherwood in Idaho—refused to heed Thompson's call and denounced the whole idea.

"It was crazy," recalled Roland. "We had just begun to organize and she wanted us to pick up and go to Washington. The militia has to build its strength locally. Linda has done some good work, but I really wish she'd be a little more disciplined and moderate in what she says."

When the Militia of Montana advised its militia network against participating in the march, Thompson denounced John Trochmann as a traitor and a government agent, a charge she continued to level at virtually every militia leader who said no to her march.

In a rambling eight-page letter that went out to militia members later in the summer, Thompson called off her march. She claimed victory. The call to arms had drawn attention to the militia movement and, she asserted, had prodded militias into organizing throughout the country. She felt that by planning the march she had accomplished another goal: "to make people realize that [an armed uprising] was a viable option."

"Has anything," she asked, "in the history of this country since the Revolutionary War, accomplished this much towards actually solving our current problems, mobilized so many, so quickly or so effectively, or done so much to literally scare the bejeebers out of the opposition, as the public announcement, by a dumpy broad from Indianapolis, that, enough is enough, we are going to arrest the traitors, man the weapons?"

She gave another reason for calling it all off: "We got word that if we did the march, the CIA was going to use bombs [around Washington] and blame it on the militia."

In reality, the aborted march destroyed Thompson's credibility among most in the militia movement. Even the extremists dismissed her as unbalanced and potentially dangerous. The ultra-right-wing John Birch Society, an ally of the militia movement, issued an official "admonition to all members and a directive to all employees" to "stay clear of her schemes."

Samuel Sherwood of the United States Militia Association in Idaho described Thompson as one of the "fruits and nuts of paranoiaville."

The episode also caused many in the patriot movement to reassess Thompson's popular Waco videos. The September 19, 1994, edition of the John Birch Society's magazine, *The New American,* called her an "insurrectionist messenger":

> It cannot be overemphasized that the case
> against the federal government for the
> Branch Davidian holocaust can be made,

> overwhelmingly, with existing reams of
> solidly documented evidence.
> Unfortunately, Thompson's videotapes
> ignore much of that evidence, focusing
> instead on sensational allegations that the
> available evidence does not convincingly
> support.

As an outsider in an outsider's movement,
Thompson continues to have a following. Her
American Justice Federation still operates one of the
militia movement's most active computer networks.
And she certainly has not backed down on any of her
demands or toned down her accusations. On May 12,
1995, Thompson was arrested again, this time for dis-
orderly conduct and resisting arrest. According to
Marion County officials, she carried a concealed gun
into the county prosecutor's office and refused to
show her permit for the weapon. As of this writing,
the charges were still pending.

The cancellation of Thompson's march did not
slow the momentum of the militia movement nationally. Several extremist militia members had run-ins
with local law enforcement, and a few were caught
planning their own violent actions.

In July 1994 federal officials uncovered a plan by a
Virginia militialike group called the Blue Ridge Hunt
Club to raid the National Guard armory in Pulaski,
Virginia. The group's leader, James Roy Mullins, was
arrested on July 27 and charged with the possession
and sale of illegal firearms and silencers. A search of
Mullins's home and a separate warehouse uncovered
thirteen guns, a quantity of explosives, hand grenades,
fuses, and blasting caps. An agent for the federal
Bureau of Alcohol, Tobacco, and Firearms said,

"Mullins is organizing a group of confederates, to be armed and trained in paramilitary fashion, in preparation for armed conflict with federal authorities should firearms legislation become too restrictive." Also found was a newsletter on computer disk that agents said detailed the group's plans. On the disk Mullins wrote, "Hit and run tactics will be our method of fighting. . . . We will destroy targets such as telephone relay centers, bridges, fuel storage tanks, communications towers, radio stations, airports, etc. . . . Human targets will be engaged . . . when it is beneficial to the cause to eliminate particular individuals who oppose us (troops, police, political figures, snitches, etc.)." As of this writing, Mullins's case is pending.

Mullins's arrest was not an isolated incident. Over the next several months, militia members in several other states had run-ins with local and federal law enforcement. Most of the incidents were relatively minor and nonviolent, but they were signs of rising tension between the growing militia movement and law enforcement agencies at the local, state, and federal levels.

Two of the most notable incidents happened in Michigan, the state with the most extensive and well-organized militia organizations.

On September 8, a police officer in Fowlerville, Michigan, stopped a car passing through town at 2:30 A.M. The three men in the vehicle were dressed in camouflage, and the police officer noticed handgun ammunition in the back of the car.

"What caught his attention right away was a loaded 9-mm clip on the back floor," recalled police chief Gary Krause.

Officers searched the car and found enough weaponry to equip a miniature army brigade: three semiautomatic 9-mm pistols, an AK–47 assault rifle, an M–1 rifle, an M–14 rifle, seven hundred rounds of ammunition, and three gas masks. The men also had two-way radios and night-vision binoculars.

Police said that two of the men identified themselves as bodyguards for Mark Koernke, a militia organizer from Dexter, Michigan. Koernke's video *America in Peril,* which detailed a massive conspiracy to turn America into a brutal dictatorship, had become an underground best-seller among militia members and others in the patriot movement throughout the country.

The men were arrested and ordered to appear in court six days later. When the court date arrived, two dozen militia members protested outside the Livingston County courthouse, where the three men were scheduled to appear.

Chief Krause said the protesters threatened police officers at the courthouse.

"They called us punks with badges. They said they wouldn't let us take their weapons again, that they'd shoot us first."

The suspects skipped their court date and were declared fugitives. Two of the men were caught, one after a lengthy car chase in a neighboring county. As of this writing, one remains at large.

The incident prompted Krause to warn, "We've got such an insurgency here that there's a very high potential of something disastrous happening."

That disaster may have been narrowly averted several months later, in another part of Michigan.

According to Eric Maloney, a former member of the Michigan Militia, twenty members of the group's Sixth Brigade plotted to blow up equipment at Camp Grayling, a National Guard base in northern

Michigan. A thirty-three-year-old auto mechanic, Maloney was a sergeant major of the Sixth Brigade at the time; he says he dropped out of the militia over the incident.

In Maloney's version of the story, an extremist faction of the Sixth Brigade had stockpiled ammonium nitrate and aluminum oxide to make a bomb—"a big bomb," said Maloney. They gathered at a Big Boy restaurant northwest of Detroit to plan the assault, which aimed to destroy Russian-made tanks on the grounds of Camp Grayling.

Maloney said that the night before the gathering at the Big Boy restaurant, he attended a public meeting of the Michigan Militia at which Mark Koernke had been a guest speaker. At that meeting, Koernke presented photos of Russian tanks being transported to Camp Grayling on rail cars, which Koernke said was evidence that foreign troops under the command of the United Nations were preparing to invade the United States. According to Maloney, Oklahoma bombing suspect Timothy McVeigh also attended the meeting at which Koernke spoke.

"McVeigh was there. My wife sat next to him. He was very attentive, very interested in that operation, volunteered his services," Maloney said, adding that McVeigh was there as a guest, not as a member of the militia. The FBI has declined to comment on whether they believe McVeigh attended the meeting.

Koernke firmly denies having seen McVeigh at the meeting and denies that he was in any way responsible for the faction's alleged decision to bomb Fort Grayling. Indeed, it is undisputed that Koernke did not attend the meeting the next day at the Big Boy restaurant where Maloney says the alleged plan to attack Fort Grayling took place.

Maloney's written summary of the plot, as reported by the *New York Times,* presents a frightening vision of a deadly battle.[1]

Maloney wrote that the group planned to

- "contact all the brigades in the state and storm Camp Grayling, killing anyone who attempts to defend the base and arresting anyone else who is left";

- "photograph, for historical purposes, all foreign equipment";

- "bring in the media" and blow up the camp "on worldwide television";

- "hunt down anyone involved in bringing in the foreign equipment and try them for war crimes in a revolutionary court, which denies the accused a chance for appeal. The accused should be executed as soon as possible";

- "hunt down all U.N. forces in the U.S."

"It was like a B movie," Maloney said. "I was unwilling to let people get killed out of stupidity."

Maloney reported the plan to the FBI on February 8, prompting an extensive investigation of the Michigan Militia. Under intense criticism from the Michigan Militia leadership, the Sixth Brigade disbanded.

---

[1] Michael Janofsky, "'Militia' Man Tells of Plot to Attack Military Base," *New York Times*, June 25, 1995, p. 14.

Another member of the brigade, Kevin Shane, has sued Maloney for slander. He charges that it was Maloney who promoted the assault. Another brigade member told the *Times* that Maloney and a brigade leader named Richard Binkley were the chief architects of the planned assault and that Maloney went to the authorities only after he and Binkley had a falling-out.

Michigan Militia commander Norman Olson calls the Camp Grayling episode "a big snafu, a big mix-up," and that Maloney "had seen or heard things that may or may not have been true." Olson and the militia leadership condemned the alleged assault plan and distanced themselves from the Sixth Brigade.

Olson said the ensuing FBI investigation turned out well for the Michigan Militia. "Whatever happened, some good came out of it. Because in February the FBI fully investigated the Michigan Militia Corps. They had a good look-see at our operation and saw we weren't breaking any laws."

But soon after the FBI investigation of the Michigan Militia, rumors of a massive federal crackdown on militias began to sweep the movement. The Internet, shortwave radio, and other militia information sources were abuzz with talk of an impending federal assault on militias throughout the country. Even the alleged date of the raid was made public by militia intelligence experts: March 25, 1995.

Rumors were so widespread that three members of Congress—Senator Larry Craig (R-Idaho), Representative Steve Stockman (R-Texas), and Representative Helen Chenoweth (R-Idaho)—wrote Attorney General Janet Reno to inquire about the pending crackdown. Reno did not respond, and paranoia gripped the movement.

On February 20 Jon Roland of the Texas Constitutional Militia sent out a communiqué to "all militia units and other patriots" that said, "By this time we have all heard the many rumors of planned federal actions against militia leaders and other patriots. A number of dates have been mentioned, and many units are on yellow alert." Roland said that the rumors may be "just patriot paranoia" or "the plans may be real." The important thing, he said, was to be ready for the worst. Across the country, militia leaders began preparing.

On March 22, Roland sent out another communiqué: "We continue to get confirming reports, but so far no hard evidence, of a mass arrest, with the date March 25 being most often mentioned. We have the NRA, other civil rights organizations, and at least six U.S. Senators inquiring into the matter."

Roland urged militia leaders to be prepared to document the raids. "If innocents, whether militia leaders or local law officials, are to be killed anyway, we need to be able to protect them and if not, to get video footage and make sure that the evidence is preserved and disseminated."

Roland also warned, "We have several reports of possible plans for atrocities to be committed by agents against innocent persons and blamed on militias." The possible "atrocity targets" included, he wrote, "crowded public places, to be bombed and the bombings blamed on militia leaders, with evidence to later be planted on them."

Was Jon Roland predicting the bombing of the Federal Building in Oklahoma City?

Just before noon on March 24, Norm Olson sent

out a communiqué warning that the coming bloodshed might be initiated by frightened militia members rather than federal agents.

"Rumor combined with our inexperience has resulted in a situation far more dangerous than a Federal sweep in the wee hours of March 25," Olson wrote in the communiqué. "My concern has been voiced to the sheriffs and to the Governor of this state. Those fears are that some frightened patriot may open fire on an unsuspecting law enforcement officer in the normal performance of his duty. WE in the patriot community must accept blame IF, repeat IF, a law enforcement officer is shot by a trembling patriot who sees sinister shadows moving in the dark."

The March 25 assault on militias didn't occur, but most militia members believed it had merely been postponed because they had found out about it. Their fears were building.

PARANOIA STRIKES DEEP

8

> **E**very government is run by liars and nothing they say should be believed.
>
> —*I. F. Stone*

> **I**t starts when you're always afraid
> Step out of line, the men come and take you away
>
> —*Stephen Stills*

Distrust of government has been a central fact of American political life since Thomas Jefferson penned the Declaration of Independence. It is healthy. The skeptical eye of the citizen gazing on the actions of governing leaders provides a check on corruption; it also makes a society less likely to blindly follow the charismatic figure who would lead us to tyranny.

But how does a healthy distrust of government mutate into the fear of black helicopters, the great strike force of the new world order, on the horizon?

Most Americans distrust the promises made by politicians and suspect that some of them are on the take, but the leading voices of the militia movement go much further: They fear that the government is preparing to wage a horrific war against ordinary

Americans. Their response is to stockpile food, first-aid supplies, and weapons—"beans, bandages, and bullets," in the words of Montana militiaman John Trochmann. By and large their fortifications are purely defensive measures to ward off the imminent assault of government forces.

To most of us, this kind of fear of a grand conspiracy seems irrational. But it is not new. In 1963 renowned historian Richard Hofstadter traced this fear through American history in an essay on what he called "the paranoid style of American politics."[1] In clinical psychology, *paranoia* refers to a mental disorder characterized by exaggeration, suspiciousness, and conspiratorial fantasy. But a "paranoid style" does not refer to the mentally ill. "It is the use of paranoid modes of expression by more or less normal people," Hofstadter wrote, "that makes the phenomenon significant." The clinically paranoid individual sees the conspiracy directed specifically at himself, whereas the politically paranoid one finds it directed at millions of others, an entire nation, a whole way of life.

Hofstadter cites examples of the paranoid style from several movements that achieved widespread acceptance—and political power—in American history. The paranoid movements saw different groups at the center of the conspiracy—the conspirators are as diverse as foreign gold traders, Masons, Catholics, Jews, Mormons, and international bankers. But the paranoid movements each believed that a well-orchestrated plan to undermine America was under way.

---

[1] Richard Hofstadter, *The Paranoid Style in American Politics and Other Essays*, (New York: Knopf, 1965), pp. 3–40.

From generation to generation, the language and world view of the paranoid style are strikingly similar, even when they represent vastly different political movements. The defining characteristics Hofstadter finds in the paranoid style are also at the heart of the conspiracy theories put forth by the leading voices of the militia movement:

- *The central conspiracy.*
  "The central image is that of a vast and sinister conspiracy, a gigantic and yet subtle machinery of influence set in motion to undermine and destroy a way of life," Hofstadter writes. In the world view of Mark Koernke, John Trochmann, and other militia leaders, this great force is the new world order, composed of top leaders in the federal government, foreign nations, international business and banking, and the United Nations.

- *An apocalyptic vision.*
  Throughout American history, the politically paranoid believed they were living at the ultimate turning point; if the great conspiracy was not stopped immediately, they thought, their whole way of life would be destroyed. "He is always manning the barricades of civilization," Hofstadter says of the politically paranoid. The militias are certainly manning the barricades, and most believe the battle is coming any day. "The only reason it hasn't happened yet," Koernke says of the new world order takeover, "is that people have risen up and taken notice."

- *A perfectly evil enemy.*
  The politically paranoid sees the world in stark
  terms of good and evil, with the enemy "a per-
  fect model of malice, a kind of amoral super-
  man." The enemy's power is vast and its
  capacity to do evil unrestrained. In Koernke's
  view, the forces of the new world order have
  already slaughtered innocents, seized control
  over the mainstream press, and developed
  means to control the minds of unsuspecting
  Americans. "This is good guys against bad guys,
  folks," says Montana militiaman Bob Fletcher,
  one of the most prolific conspiracy researchers
  in the movement.

- *Obsessive fact-gathering.*
  The politically paranoid is an exhaustive
  researcher, feverishly compiling pages and
  pages of "evidence" to prove the vast conspiracy. "The very fantastic character of [his] conclusions leads to heroic strivings for 'evidence'
  to prove that the unbelievable is the only thing
  to be believed," Hofstadter writes. The mantra
  of the militia conspiracy theorists is "We've got
  the documents." Militia researchers use their
  "documents"—which include news clippings,
  anonymous reports from other researchers,
  official government statements, letters from
  high places, fuzzy photographs, etc.—to put
  together the pieces of the conspiracy. It all fits
  together; there are no loose ends. In June 1995
  Norman Olson of the Michigan Militia submit-
  ted to Congress a three-ring binder packed
  with over eight hundred pages of "documents"
  proving a vast conspiracy to undermine the

Constitution and deprive Americans of basic liberties.

The militia researchers often compile reliable information about government actions, but they make what Hofstadter calls "a curious leap in imagination" to conclude that the evidence "proves" an overarching conspiracy. Sometimes, however, the evidence itself is highly questionable. For example, a central piece of evidence cited by John Trochmann is the back of a Kix cereal box. The box depicts a map of America divided into eleven regions—from "the Pacific Coast" to "New England"—and urges kids to "explore this great land of ours!" A photocopy of the cereal box's back panel is distributed in Militia of Montana information kits with the handwritten caption, "1994 KIX CERIAL [sic] BOX BACK. THE SAME EXACT MAP AS 1986 T.V. SERIES AMERIKA." Trochmann says the map is the same one used in *Amerika*, a 1986 TV movie about a fictional Russian takeover of the United States. He somehow concludes that the Kix map is yet another piece of evidence that the new world order is planning to take over America and divide it into the very regions depicted on both the cereal box and in the TV series *Amerika*.

The paranoid style may produce irrational fears and fantastic notions of impending doom, but that does not mean it is devoid of logic. In fact, the paranoid world view may actually be *more logical* than the real world. In the real world, events are often driven by chance, luck, mistakes, failures, or ambiguities. It is often impossible to pinpoint why things turn out the way they do. But for the conspiratorial mind-set, *nothing* happens by accident. The enemy is too powerful for that. Virtually all significant events fit into a central theme; the trick for the researcher is to put the pieces together.

At the time Hofstadter wrote his essay, the paranoid style dominated the far right in American politics. Starting with McCarthyism in the 1950s, the far right saw a vast conspiracy to turn the United States over to our Communist enemies in the Soviet Union. Senator Joseph McCarthy described the situation in stark terms:

> How can we account for our present situation unless we believe that men high in this government are concerting to deliver us to disaster? This must be the product of a great conspiracy, a conspiracy on a scale so immense as to dwarf any previous such venture in the history of man. A conspiracy of infamy so black that, when it is finally exposed, its principals shall be forever deserving of the maledictions of all honest men. [2]

Following McCarthy's downfall, the mantle of right-wing paranoia fell to Robert H. Welch, Jr., and his John Birch Society. Hofstadter quotes Welch as saying in 1960, "Communist influences are now in almost complete control of our government." At the time of Hofstadter's writing, the John Birch Society was in its heyday, reaching a membership of more than 150,000. They represented a paranoid style that reached a vocal minority of the American people. Hofstadter offers the example of Republican senator

---

[2] *Congressional Record*, 82nd Congress, first session (June 14, 1951), p. 6602.

Thomas R. Kuchel, who reported in July 1963 that of the sixty thousand letters he received each month, 10 percent were what he called "fright mail"—anguished letters about "the latest *PLOT!!* to OVERTHROW America!!!" The letters sounded remarkably like the mailings of the Militia of Montana and the content of Mark Koernke's *The Intelligence Report*.

> Some of the more memorable "plots" that come to mind include these: 35,000 Communist Chinese troops bearing arms and wearing deceptively dyed powder-blue uniforms are poised on the Mexican border, about to invade San Diego; the United States has turned over—or will at any moment—its Army, Navy, and Air Force to the command of a Russian colonel in the United Nations; almost every well-known American or free-world leader is, in reality, a top Communist agent; a United States Army guerrilla-warfare exercise in Georgia, called Water Moccasin III, is in actuality a United Nations operation preparatory to taking over our country.[3]

After Hofstadter wrote his essay on the paranoid style, America underwent the mass upheavals of the Vietnam War era. The paranoid style became a dominant characteristic of the far left in American politics (the paranoid right didn't disappear; it was just drowned out by the louder political noises of the

---

[3] Quoted by Hofstadter from the *New York Times*, July 21, 1963, VI, p. 6.

1960s). The Creedence Clearwater Revival song "Bad Moon Rising" captured the mood:

> Hope you are quite prepared to die
> Looks like we're in for nasty weather

Sixties radicals—personified in the antiwar movement and groups ranging from Tom Hayden's Students for a Democratic Society to the Weather Underground—brought intense distrust of government into the cultural mainstream. "Question authority" became the mantra of the movement that set out to discredit the government, and with it a whole social order, which the young radicals believed had become an oppressive police state. As evidence that the government had become an evil force, they pointed to the Vietnam War, to racial oppression, and, after 1970, to the four protesters gunned down by National Guard troops at Kent State University.

"What happened in the 1960s was that the government was successfully delegitimated," says Professor Gerald Marwell, a sociologist at the University of Wisconsin. "We had a period from World War II through the 1950s where the government was seen as having rescued the nation from the Depression and successfully prosecuted the war, and then we were told in the 1960s that the emperor has no clothes and people shouldn't accept what they are told."

Professor Marwell adds, "And rather than going away, that sensibility has grown over the past thirty years." In its purest form, it is found in the militia movement.

During the upheavals of the sixties, many who are now in the militia movement were fighting in

Vietnam. Many of them scorned the antiwar protesters as unpatriotic traitors. Now they believe they have much more in common with the sixties radicals than with the government they served during the war.

"Those protesters of the sixties and seventies that I looked down my nose on, were Americans that were trying to expose the evil in our government," says Michigan Militia cofounder Ray Southwell. "And I looked down my nose on them. So today Americans look down their nose on me. I now understand what they went through in the sixties."

"The patriot movement of thirty years ago was absolutely right," says Montana militiaman Bob Fletcher. "The Vietnam war was a lying, fraudulent, disgusting thing."

Left-wing paranoia hit full stride in the 1980s with a group called the Christic Institute. The brainchild of 1960s antiwar veteran Daniel Sheehan, the Christic Institute's mission was to effect social change through litigation. In the early 1970s, Sheehan, a Harvard graduate, had done pro bono work to defend the Black Panthers and rioting prison inmates. He was on the five-lawyer team that defended the *New York Times* in the Pentagon Papers case and, as an attorney of the American Civil Liberties Union, he defended Native Americans who had been at Wounded Knee. He even spent a year working for the flamboyant criminal defense lawyer F. Lee Bailey. With the Christic Institute, Sheehan was prepared to take on the very source of evil in the United States: the government.

In 1986 Sheehan went to court to prove that the

United States had been corrupted by a grand conspiracy that dated back to the 1963 assassination of President John F. Kennedy. In a forty-five-page affidavit filed in a Florida federal court, Sheehan charged that a "secret team" has been in control of the federal government since the Kennedy assassination. The secret team was allegedly made up of CIA agents, businessmen from several nations, Colombian cocaine kingpins, and military leaders, including retired general Richard Secord. In an elaborate lawsuit, the Christic Institute set out to sue the secret team. His suit targeted twenty-nine former U.S. intelligence and military personnel.

"By definition," Sheehan's affidavit charged, "these defendants, alleged merchants of heroin and terrorism, are organized criminals on a scale larger than life."

Sheehan's secret-team theory exemplified another common characteristic of political paranoia in American history: optimism. Although the paranoid conspiracy theories are laced with pessimism about powerful forces of evil and impending doom, they also represent a hopeful optimism. If so much evil can be traced to a central conspiracy, then evil can be eliminated by defeating the conspiracy. With a single lawsuit, Sheehan hoped to zap the force behind such tragedies and scandals as the Vietnam War, the Kennedy assassinations, Watergate, and the murder sprees of drug cartels.

The Iran-contra scandal was just coming to light as Sheehan and Christic's team of lawyers pursued the case and provided additional evidence for the secret-team theory. The case cost approximately $40,000 a week for the Christic Institute to maintain, but Sheehan's sweeping allegations, combined with outrage over Iran-contra, brought a steady stream of supporters. Rock star Jackson Browne performed a benefit concert to fund Sheehan's efforts.

In February 1989 a U.S. District Court judge tossed the secret-team lawsuit out of court and ordered the Christic Institute to pay one million dollars for filing what the judge called a case based on "unsubstantiated rumor and speculation."

Sheehan's effort was running on empty. He closed Christic's office on Capitol Hill in Washington and faded into obscurity. But his secret-team theory was alive and well, kept going by scores of conspiracy researchers around the country. Parts of the theory were popularized by Oliver Stone's 1991 hit movie *JFK.*

Bob Fletcher was one of those who worked with the Christic Institute. Fletcher is convinced that the secret-team theory was "dead right"; getting thrown out of court was just another element of the conspiracy.

Today, Fletcher is a spokesman and "investigator" for the Militia of Montana and a big hit on the militia lecture circuit nationwide. Like several other leading figures in the militia movement, he sees himself as continuing the work of the Christic Institute. Texas militia leader Jon Roland says of the Christic Institute, "We think they were on to something and I have a lot of respect for them." Roland's own conspiracy research is strikingly similar to Sheehan's. The primary difference is that Roland uses the term "shadow government" instead of "secret team" to describe the forces that are taking over the government.

In the world of the politically paranoid, political distinctions seem to melt away. The Christic Institute came from the far left of American politics and the militia movement comes out of the far right, but their conclusions are almost identical. Indeed, the militia conspiracy theorists have more in common with the left-wing activists of the Christic Institute than they do with the conservative wing of the Republican Party.

Ronald Reagan and Oliver North, for example, are heroes to many right-wing conservatives, but to Fletcher, Roland, Koernke, and many other militia leaders, they represent evil as much as or more than any liberal Democrat.

"We don't want to hear about left and right, conservative and liberal, all these bullshit labels. Let's get back to the idea of good guys and bad guys, righteous government," says Fletcher, who ran for Congress in 1990 as a Democrat. Fletcher won the Democratic nomination and, with a poorly financed campaign based on conspiracy theories, won 40 percent of the vote. His opponent was conservative Florida Republican Bill McCollum.

Writing in the *New Yorker,* Michael Kelly argued that political labels lose meaning in the world of the politically paranoid. "There is no left and no right here," Kelly wrote, "only unanimity of belief in the boundless, cabalistic evil of the government and its allies." He calls the phenomenon "fusion paranoia."[4]

In less extreme forms, fusion paranoia permeates America's political culture. While only a small minority of Americans believes the conspiracy theories of Bob Fletcher or Daniel Sheehan, most of us have a sense that government is no longer controlled by the average citizen. A 1991 study by the Kettering

---

[4] Michael Kelly, "The Road to Paranoia," in the *New Yorker,* June 19, 1995, pp. 60–75.

Foundation revealed the depths of popular disgust with politics. Kettering's president, David Mathews, summed up the study's findings:

> People talk as though our political system had been taken over by alien beings. Many Americans do not believe they are living in a democracy now! . . . They don't believe the average citizen even influences, much less rules. . . . They point their fingers at politicians, at powerful lobbyists, and— this came as a surprise—the media. They see these three groups as a political class, the rulers of an oligarchy that has replaced democracy.

The findings of the Kettering study reveal the legitimate discontent with the federal government felt by most Americans. Fletcher and other militia leaders simply push that discontent to extreme levels.

It is important to note that not all militia members believe the far-out conspiracy theories of people such as Koernke, Fletcher, and Linda Thompson. Many militia members represent the mainstream discontent reflected in the Kettering study, and others are active because of a more narrowly defined concern about gun control. It's easy to dismiss the paranoid extremists, but the discontent driving the militia movement is real and extends far beyond the membership of citizens' militias.

When fear of a federal crackdown gripped the militia movement in March 1995, Michigan Militia leader Norman Olson spoke out against the "peddlers of paranoia." In a letter to *Soldier of Fortune* magazine, Olson wrote:

The fertile ground of the fears and imagination of the patriot community has been prepared by those who have spent their time talking about "black helicopters" and armies of Russian soldiers hiding in America. Several radio talk people, underground newspapers, and peddlers of books and video tapes have grown rich by pandering to an eager market of people frightened by things that go bump in the night. Now those same frightened people, already at the limits of rational thought, are given the powerful suggestion that a massive Federal raid will commence just hours from now. With that, these frightened people are becoming a threat to themselves and the patriot cause. One accident could trigger an incident that would be very damaging to the cause.

Olson warned that paranoia was so high that frightened militia members might start shooting; law enforcement officers could come under fire by "a trembling patriot who sees sinister shadows moving in the dark."

Olson's warning is an eerie reminder that extreme paranoia can have deadly consequences.

THE RACIST FRINGE

9

There is no way a society based on Aryan values and an Aryan outlook can evolve peacefully from a society which has succumbed to Jewish spiritual corruption.

—*William Pierce,*
The Turner Diaries

"But *who* are you?"

The man on the other end of the phone wanted to know if I was pure enough to talk to Richard Butler, the seventy-six-year-old patriarch of the Aryan Nations.

Refusing to play by his rules, I repeated my request to speak with the old man who presides over the six-building compound in Hayden Lake, Idaho, that serves as the home to a microscopic sect of hard-core racists.

"I mean, *who* are you? You're asking to talk to our führer, the leader of our movement. He's a very busy man."

When I explained that I was a reporter, the man quickly handed the phone to Butler. I guess even the führer likes to see his name in the paper.

Richard Butler is a demonic man, but not overly

influential. He spews a dull message of hate that reaches a pathetically small crowd of ten to twenty-five people at "church services" each Sunday. The sign beside the gravel driveway that leads to his shabby mecca reads *Whites Only.* Swastikas and portraits of Adolf Hitler adorn the walls of the main building, a wooden hut. At the main entrance to the "chapel," there is a poster of Hitler with the caption "When I Come Back, No More Mister Nice Guy." Each July, Butler holds the World Conference of the Aryan Nations, when about two hundred racists emerge to share messages of race war.

Butler's message doesn't have to reach many people to do a great deal of damage. He has already managed to inspire violence. In 1984, a group called the Order pulled off a couple of armored-truck heists that netted them almost $4 million, stockpiled enough weapons to supply a small army, and assassinated Denver talk show host Alan Berg. The Order was led by Robert Jay Matthews, a follower of Richard Butler and his Aryan Nations.

Butler despises more than Jews, African-Americans, and homosexuals. Richard Butler says he also hates the militia movement.

"They are not for the preservation of the white race, which means they are in line with government policy. They're actually traitors to the white race; they seek to integrate with blacks, Jews, and others," Butler said in a quiet, gruff voice. "I think they are a government-sponsored movement, maybe the CIA."

As an afterthought he added: "A lot of people are white on the outside but black on the inside with a Jewish brain."

He does not rage, or even raise his voice, when he gives this message of racial hatred. Rather, he sounds bored.

Early media reports repeatedly tied the militia movement to the Aryan Nations and other white-supremacist groups. These reports painted the militias as the 1990s incarnation of earlier paramilitary groups, such as the Ku Klux Klan, which armed themselves for racial terrorism and war.

One reason for the tie-in to white supremacists was Militia of Montana leader John Trochmann. One of the most influential figures in the movement, Trochmann had been a guest at the Hayden Lake headquarters of the Aryan Nations and was even a featured speaker at their 1990 World Congress. Trochmann maintained that he had never joined the group and had used his speech to denounce their "immorality." But Butler said that Trochmann had expressed support for the Aryan Nations' goals.

The militias seemed to share at least some things in common with the earlier armed racist groups. When the KKK first formed in the 1860s, for example, it was described as an organization dedicated to community defense—kind of like the "giant neighborhood watch" that Trochmann calls the militias. It was to be the enforcer, not the breaker, of laws and the defender of the weak and innocent.

At a KKK convention in 1867 in Nashville, Tennessee, the Klan set forth an agenda that is remarkably similar to the rhetoric of the militia groups of the 1990s. "With much talk of unity of purpose, concert of action, proper limits, and authority to the prudent, a constitution or prescript was drawn up," writes historian David Chalmers. "The weak, innocent, defenseless, and oppressed, the

Constitution of the United States, and all constitutional laws were to be upheld."[1]

The South was in near chaos following the Civil
War, and in many areas the Klan was welcomed as a
civic organization. Of course, it soon turned into a
murderous gang bent on lynching blacks, Catholics,
and whites who got in their way. The "neighborhood
watch" managed to become the neighborhood's worst
enemy.

In the late 1970s and early 1980s, an armed offshoot of the KKK formed and called itself Posse
Comitatus, which is Latin for "power of the county."
In words that echo some elements of the militia movement, the group declared all governments above the
county level to be illegitimate. Over the past couple of
years, former Posse Comitatus leader James
Wickstrom has been busily working the militia circuit.
He has attended militia meetings in Pennsylvania, and
his "intelligence reports" have been distributed
through the Internet on multiple militia newsgroups
and have also made their way into militia newsletters.

In the June 1, 1995, issue of the militia-friendly
newsletter *Of, By & For the People,* Wickstrom
warned that a cabal of "international central bankers"
has "vomited its stench all over this once great
Christian Republic. . . . Even aliens have more Rights
than natural born citizens." The only way to fight this
"police/slave state government structure," he wrote,
is through armed resistance: "The battle will not be
won at the voting machine. You know this and so do
I. 'We the People' will take back this Christian

---

[1] David M. Chalmers, *Hooded Americanism: The History
of the Ku Klux Klan* (New York: Franklin Watts, 1951),
p. 9.

Republic, one way or another. But get ready, it's very close. What side of the 'line' are you on?"

The Aryan Nations, Posse Comitatus, and other militant racist groups have for decades labeled their common enemy "Zionist Occupational Government," or ZOG. For the racist extremists, ZOG is a Jewish-organized conspiracy on a grand scale, controlling the United Nations, most of the federal government, the media, and the "international bankers" who they say control the Federal Reserve. Most of the conspiracy theories that whirl about the militia movement see the same evil cabal of bankers, politicians, and the media—but without the reference to ZOG or Jewish control. Many in the militia movement who believe these theories appear to be unaware that they were first put forth by white supremacists.

Some observers of the extremist groups in the United States say militant racist groups are attempting to use the militia movement to gain new, and very well armed, converts to their cause. "They're using oppressive big government as the come-on," says a former Idaho priest who once had his house bombed by neo-Nazis. "It's a new hook, a new way to recruit people and get attention. But I don't think people like John Trochmann have changed their thoughts and ideology."

Journalist Chip Berlet says the strategy is working. "They are finding fertile ground for this effort," Berlet says of the white supremacists, because conspiracy theories rampant in the militia movement "are simply an updated and expanded variation of conspiracy theories long promoted by far-right paramilitary organizations." Berlet tracks the far right for the Boston think tank Political Research Associates and was one of the first to extensively study the militia movement.

The decentralized cell structure of many militias—
most notably the Militia of Montana—makes it very
difficult to measure the inroads made by racist groups
into the militia movement. The M.O.M. handbook
proposes a militia organization through highly secretive seven-person cells. Public militias, such as those
in Michigan and Texas, have open meetings and open
membership, and they disavow racism. But with tiny,
clandestine cells such as those of the Militia of
Montana, it's nearly impossible to gauge who is
involved and what their beliefs are.

Before founding M.O.M., Trochmann joined with
former KKK Grand Dragon Louis Beam to start a
group called United Citizens for Justice. The group's
stated purpose was to protest federal actions in the
1992 Randy Weaver incident. They pushed to have
criminal charges filed against the federal agents
involved and raised money to pay for Weaver's legal
fees.

At the time, Beam, who is now the "special ambassador" to the Aryan Nations, was also pushing what
he called "leaderless resistance" to the federal government. In an Illinois publication called *The War Eagle:
A Voice and Forum for Revolutionary Pan-Aryanism*,
Beam explained how individuals should work through
"phantom cells" that act independently to achieve
common goals.

> Organs of information distribution such as
> newspapers, leaflets, computers, etc.,
> which are widely available to all, keep
> each person informed of events, allowing
> for a planned response that will take many
> variations. . . . No one need issue an order
> to anyone. Those idealists truly committed

to the cause of freedom will act when they
feel the time is ripe, or will take their cue
from others who preceded them.

Although Beam has never been publicly affiliated
with the Militia of Montana, Trochmann's proposed
seven-man cells seem uncomfortably similar to
Beam's concept of "leaderless resistance." And the
M.O.M. headquarters in Noxon certainly serves as a
network of information distribution capable of keeping "each person informed of events," as Beam
instructs.

In addition to Trochmann, another influential militia
figure in Montana is M. J. "Red" Beckman of Billings.
His 1984 book, *The Church Deceived*, describes Jews
as followers of Satan who control "our government,
our major media, our banks and legal profession." He
writes: "They talk about the terrible holocaust of
Hitler's Nazi Germany. Was that not a judgment
upon a people who believe Satan is their god?"

But it is also clear that most militia organizers are
intolerant of white supremacists in their midst. The
Pittsburgh Post-Gazette reported that James
Wickstrom was thrown out of a militia meeting in
western Pennsylvania because of his views. And
Texas militia leader Jon Roland, who has confronted
Wickstrom's views on the Internet, says, "He knows
that I won't tolerate his rhetoric."

"I think there are two movements out there," says
Henry McDaniel, the editor of an on-line computer magazine for militias called the *Journal for Patriot Justice*.
"One is racist and one is not." McDaniel, who is one
of a growing number of blacks in the patriot movement, rails against racism in the militias with as much
conviction as he rails against the federal government.

One of the increasingly popular militia leaders is
James Johnson, a black man from an inner-city area of
Columbus, Ohio. A thirty-three-year-old employee of
a utility company, Johnson first came to national
prominence in December 1994, when he appeared on
the *Donahue* show with Trochmann, Norm Olson of
the Michigan Militia, and two other militia leaders.
Since then he has testified before Congress and
become a regular guest on shortwave radio programs
that champion militias. An impassioned and eloquent
speaker, he is also a frequent guest speaker at militia-
related events beyond Ohio.

At a June 1995 gun-rights rally in Washington,
D.C., Johnson put his arm around John Trochmann's
wife, Carolyn, and told the crowd, "Now, I'm getting
sick and tired of people calling us Klansmen."

Johnson and his wife, Helen, who is white, are veterans of Ross Perot's 1992 campaign for the presi-
dency. In addition to the militia, they have started a
group called E Pluribus Unum. The group acts as an
information clearinghouse for militias, publishing a
newsletter and sponsoring guest speakers such as
Michigan militiaman Mark Koernke.

"It's just not accurate to call them armed Nazis,"
Berlet says of the militia movement. "Even when they
espouse theories that originate from white
supremacists, most of these people do not see themselves as racists or anti-Semites."

The militant racists exist at the fringes of the militia movement and are not welcomed by its mainstream leadership. But, Berlet reminds us, "there have
long been paramilitary groups who have advocated
race war in America."

For would-be race warriors, the vision of their
future battle is presented in a novel called *The Turner*

Diaries, written by William L. Pierce under the pseudonym Andrew MacDonald. The book has sold more than 190,000 copies since it was first published in 1978. Pierce is a former leader of the American Nazi Party and now heads up his own neo-Nazi organization, called the National Alliance. Before he entered the hate-filled world of white supremacy, Pierce climbed the ranks of academia. A graduate of Rice University, he received his Ph.D. in physics from the University of Colorado in 1962. He then taught physics at Oregon State University for three years before joining George Lincoln Rockwell's American Nazi Party.

In the catalogue through which he sells *The Turner Diaries* and other publications, Pierce warns that the novel "will be too strong a dish for any reader who has not thoroughly prepared himself for it." As preliminary readings, he recommends dozens of other books, including Adolf Hitler's *Mein Kampf.*

The Turner Diaries is cast in the future as the newly discovered diary of Earl Turner, a member of an underground white supremacist group called the Organization. After the passage of "the Cohen Act," which outlawed private gun ownership, the Organization rises up against "the Jewish-liberal-democratic-equalitarian plague" to establish an all-white "New Era" at the end of the twentieth century. Banding together through clandestine cells, the Organization slaughters Jews and blacks and raises money by robbing Jewish merchants.

Writing in his diary, the narrator explains why the murderous spree is necessary: "There is no way a society based on Aryan values and an Aryan outlook can evolve peacefully from a society which has succumbed to Jewish spiritual corruption."

As the Organization solidifies control over different parts of the country, they expel the blacks they don't kill to government-held areas. Others who are not sufficiently Aryan are herded into canyons and slaughtered.

The excruciatingly violent narrative builds up to a grisly day of reckoning.

"Today has been the Day of Rope—a grim and bloody day, but an unavoidable one," the narrator writes. Blacks, Jews, and white "race traitors" are executed en masse.

> At practically every street corner I passed this evening on my way to HQ there was a dangling corpse, four at every intersection. Hanging from a single overpass only about a mile from here is a group of about 30, each with an identical placard around its neck bearing the printed legend, "I betrayed my race." Two or three of the group had been decked out in academic robes before they were strung up, and the whole batch are apparently faculty members from the nearby U.C.L.A. campus.

He continues:

> There were many thousands of female corpses like that in the city tonight, all wearing placards around their necks. They are the white women who were married to or living with blacks, with Jews, or with other nonwhite males.

The other whites hung during the Day of Rope are "the politicians, the lawyers, the businessmen, the TV newscasters, the newspaper reporters and editors, the judges, the teachers, the school officials, the 'civic leaders,' the bureaucrats, the preachers and all the others who, for reasons of career or status or votes or whatever, helped implement the System's racial program."

In the end, the Organization wins its battle against the government when the hero makes a suicide nuclear bomb attack on the Pentagon in a small airplane. The all-white "New Era" dawns in America.

The Turner Diaries was a favorite of Oklahoma bombing suspect Timothy McVeigh, according to Roger Barnett, who served with him in the Army at Fort Riley in Kansas. Barnett drove the Bradley fighting vehicle on which McVeigh served as a gunner. Others say McVeigh frequently sold copies of the book at gun shows.

"He carried that book all the time," one gun collector told the *New York Times*. "He sold it at the shows. He'd have a few copies in the cargo pocket of his cammies. They were supposed to be ten dollars, but he'd sell them for five dollars. It was like he was looking for converts." [2]

McVeigh's interest in *The Turner Diaries* is not unusual. After all, the book has sold nearly 200,000 copies.

But there is something eerie about McVeigh's apparent fascination with the book.

On page 42, the Organization carries out its first act of war against the government. Immediately

---

[2] "Bomb Suspect Felt at Home Riding the Gun-Show Circuit," *New York Times*, July 2, 1995, p. A1.

following the passage of the Cohen Act, which out-lawed guns, the hero uses a truck bomb—made with a mix of fertilizer and fuel oil strikingly similar to the one used in the Oklahoma bombing—to destroy a federal building, the FBI headquarters in Washington, D.C.

With the bombing, the Organization begins its war on the federal government.

These people are killers.
They must be treated like
killers.

—President Bill Clinton,
April 19, 1995

PANIC IN
THE
MOVEMENT 10

On April 19, 1995, a horrified
nation witnessed the deadliest act of terrorism in
American history. Detonating at 9:02 A.M., a bomb
ripped through the nine-story Alfred P. Murrah
Federal Building in Oklahoma City just as parents
were showing up for work and dropping their children
off at the second-floor day care center. The heat from
the explosion was so intense that some of the victims
were nearly vaporized; the rest were crushed beneath
tons of shattered glass, bricks, steel, concrete, and
other debris. The terror struck America's heartland,
killing 168 people with a single act of defiance.

While local firemen and rescue workers heroically
pulled survivors from the rubble, the rest of the country went searching for someone to blame. Who could
have perpetrated such a heinous crime?

President Clinton vowed to hunt down the "evil cowards" responsible for the attack. Expressing the emotions of millions of Americans, he declared, "These people are killers and must be treated like killers." Attorney General Janet Reno said the perpetrators would face the death penalty when caught.

Immediately fingers pointed to the Middle East. CNN reported that two men "of Middle Eastern appearance" were seen fleeing the scene. The FBI detained a Jordanian-American man in Chicago—he had flown out of Oklahoma City shortly after the blast and was on his way out of the country. In an interview with CBS News just hours after the bombing, former Oklahoma congressman Dave McCurdy said there was "very clear evidence" that "fundamentalist Islamic terrorist groups" were behind the attack.

It wasn't surprising that the first leads pointed to the Middle East. Arab terrorists had carried out similar bombings in Beirut, Buenos Aires, and Lebanon. Arab terrorists were also charged with the 1993 World Trade Center bombing in New York and the 1988 bombing of Pan Am Flight 103 over Lockerbie, Scotland.

But militia members around the country sensed that the April 19 bombing had nothing to do with Arab terrorists. The date of the bombing was simply too significant to be a coincidence.

"It's about Waco," Colorado militiaman Ron Cole told the *Boulder Weekly* while CNN was still hot on the trail of men of Middle Eastern appearance. "The Oklahoma bombing was a very cold, eye-for-an-eye, tooth-for-a-tooth action of retaliation. I abhor it, but now I have to deal with it realistically."

Exactly one year earlier, on April 19, 1994, the federal siege of the Branch Davidian compound in

Waco, Texas, had ended with a mighty firestorm that killed seventy-four people. Like so many others, Cole had joined the militia movement because of Waco. He had even produced a videotape and written a book that put forth the common militia view that the government committed cold-blooded, premeditated murder in Waco.

"I personally consider myself exceptionally responsible for this bombing, in that I've put out more information about what happened in Waco than anyone on earth," Cole said. "I can only imagine the guys who did this sitting there reading my book, watching my video, and getting so enraged that they were thinking about what they might blow up in retaliation."

A plethora of federal agencies had offices in the Oklahoma City federal building, including the Bureau of Alcohol, Tobacco, and Firearms—the agency that spearheaded the Waco raid.

On the day of the bombing, militia leader Mark Koernke opened his shortwave radio program, *The Intelligence Report,* with reference to another significant event in American history that occurred on April 19: "Good evening, ladies and gentlemen. . . . It is the nineteenth of April, 1995, two hundred and twenty years after the shot heard round the world. The horses have already ridden across the countryside. The battles for Lexington and Concord have taken place today, and the British are now in Boston, licking their wounds, ladies and gentlemen." Koernke then reminded listeners of the Waco anniversary, saying of Attorney General Reno, "The Butcher of Waco got away with murder!"

But Koernke wasn't saying that the bombing was the work of the militias. Rather, he insisted, it was the work of those people within the federal government and the United Nations who had set out to destroy America: "It is yet another foot-stomp on the part of the new world order crowd to manipulate the population."

Koernke was among the first to charge that the federal government was behind the bombing, but he wasn't alone. Within hours of the bombing, militia discussion groups on the computer Internet—most notably "misc.activism.militia" and "talk.politics.guns"—were full of talk about the bombing.

Just hours after the bombing, an Internet message entitled "OK City bombed by FBI" set the tone:

> If this turns out to be a bomb, expect them
> to tie it to the militia. Waco tie-in. I have
> expected this to come before now. I will
> lodge a prediction here. They will try to tie
> it to Waco. Janet Reno is behind this, the
> campaign will succeed because the media
> will persuade the public. Expect a crack-
> down. Bury your guns and use the codes.
> This puts us back another 20 years. It
> shouldn't come as a surprise.

Panic began to rock the militia movement as rumors spread that the bombing would be blamed on the militias and used as an excuse for the ruthless federal crackdown they had long feared was coming.

Meanwhile, the FBI had dispatched its top forensic experts to probe the wreckage in Oklahoma City for clues. The team, led by Special Agent James Lyons, had investigated the World Trade Center bombing in February 1993. In just sixteen hours Lyons's team came up with a crucial piece of evidence: the mangled remains of an axle from a 1993 Ford truck. The axle had the vehicle identification number, a crucial bit of information that enabled the FBI, with the help of Ford Motor Company, to track down the truck they believe carried the explosives. It was a Ryder truck that had been rented from Elliot's Body Shop in Junction City, Kansas.

Shortly after dawn on April 20, FBI agents approached the owner of Elliot's. Based on his detailed description of the men who rented the truck, the FBI produced a composite drawing of the suspects. By midafternoon the drawings of the two suspects, labeled John Doe No. 1 and John Doe No. 2 because their true identities were unknown, were being broadcast by television stations across the country and around the world.

By all appearances, the suspects were Americans.

What authorities didn't know was that one of their prime suspects, John Doe No. 1, was already in an Oklahoma jail. Just ninety minutes after the bombing, state trooper Charles Hanger had pulled over Timothy McVeigh for speeding on Interstate 35, about sixty miles north of Oklahoma City. McVeigh's beat-up Mercury Marquis had no license plate. When Hanger approached the car, he noticed McVeigh's shoulder holster and saw that he was carrying a 9-mm Glock semiautomatic pistol. The gun, like the car, was unregistered. It was also loaded with hollow-point "cop killer" bullets. Hanger arrested McVeigh and brought him to the jail in Perry, Oklahoma.

For two days, the police kept McVeigh in jail, not connecting the quiet prisoner with the FBI sketch. Five minutes before he was due to go before the Noble County court, where he probably would have been released on $500 bail, local prosecutors received

a call from the FBI telling them to hang on to
McVeigh. The FBI believed McVeigh was their man.
Soon afterward they arrested Terry and James
Nichols. Eventually McVeigh and Terry Nichols were
charged with the blast.

As reporters interviewed countless acquaintances
of the suspects, a vivid portrait of the accused terrorists emerged. Former army buddies, they harbored an
intense hatred of the federal government. Nichols had
attempted to renounce his citizenship and declare
himself "sovereign." McVeigh had repeatedly watched
Linda Thompson's videos on the federal siege of
Waco and was so enraged by what happened to the
Branch Davidians that he had driven to Waco months
after the fire to view the burned-out wreckage. Then
came the "connection"—the suspects reportedly "had
ties" to the Michigan Militia.

Americans were horrified to see that the alleged
terrorists behind the Oklahoma bombing were fellow
Americans. *Time* magazine expressed the shock felt
by millions of Americans:

> The truck bomb in the heartland brought
> the terrible realization that America has
> bred its own sort of new political monster,
> one afflicted with hatred so malignant that
> only murder on a grand scale can satisfy it.
> Who really knows how many citizens—a
> dozen? a hundred?—feel so passionately
> that their government is the Great Satan
> that they would resort to such evil? This
> much is certain: the courage of the
> bereaved and the heroism of the rescuers
> in Oklahoma City are the stuff of true
> patriotism.

In seeking out the "political monster," *Time* magazine, and almost every major media outlet in the
United States, descended upon the militias. The mainstream media had paid scant attention to militias
before the bombing, but now they were on the front
page of virtually every daily newspaper in the country.
Hundreds, probably thousands, of reporters probed
the "connection" between the bombing and the militia
movement.

James McQuaid of the Michigan Militia tried in
vain to defuse the situation with this statement:

> Approximately one month ago, one of the
> Nichols brothers came to a militia meet-
> ing (which are open to the public).
> During the open forum part of the meet-
> ing, Mr. Nichols specifically indicated
> that he was not a member of any militia
> unit. Mr. Nichols encouraged those pre-
> sent at the meeting to 'cut up their
> driver's licenses.' In addition, Mr.
> Nichols sought to promote a discussion of
> tax protester issues and attempted to dis-
> tribute tax resister material printed by
> someone from Minnesota and was asked
> to leave the meeting. The militia leader I
> spoke with indicated that this was their
> only contact with either of the Nichols
> brothers.

As the media frenzy heated up, many militia members ran for cover, refusing to talk to the press.
Almost all of those who spoke to reporters condemned the bombing and reaffirmed what they had
always said before: The militias are self-defense

groups, not terrorist organizations. From the start, most believed the bombing was a federal government plot designed to discredit the militias and provide an excuse for a crackdown.

Ron Cole was one of the few militia members to say that the bombing had come out of the movement. "We may not like what they did, but they took it upon themselves to commit an act," Cole told the *Boulder Weekly*. "Up until now, militia members and federal authorities have been staring at each other across an open field, through binoculars, waiting for something to happen. On April 19, 1995, someone within our ranks threw a grenade."

Cole's message to fellow militia members was to condemn the bombing but not to give up the fight. "You may not like the horror that resulted from the act, but you can't just wave white flags and surrender because someone on your side committed a violent act without orders. We all reject the tactics used by these people, but you don't give up the war."

At first the main focus was on the Michigan Militia. As militiaman Ray Southwell put it, "After the Oklahoma bombing, the national press corps attacked the Michigan Militia Corps."

As reports of the bombing suspect's ties to the militias dominated the news, sixty militia leaders, dressed in combat camouflage, assembled at Fort John Williams, their militia-made training camp on a sprawling backwoods farm in northern Michigan. The fort was highly defensible—it was surrounded by hand-dug trenches and ridges overlooking steep wooded valleys, and it was several miles from the nearest paved road. It was April 23, and rescue workers were still desperately searching for survivors in the rubble in Oklahoma City. The Michigan Militia dug in, petrified at the prospect of a federal crackdown in response to the bombing.

"The fear level is heightened right now, but it would be absolutely foolish for the government to attack us," Southwell told the crowd of reporters that journeyed out to Fort John Williams.

He predicted what would happen in the coming weeks: "Citizens will want more of our freedoms restricted. Freedom of speech will end. Federal legislation will curtail freedoms, which will be rapidly eroded. There will be an attempt to shut down the militias."

The Michigan Militia welcomed the throngs of reporters and television crews that camped out in front of their fort. The government "would not dare to violate the Bill of Rights" with an attack while television cameras were there to record the scene.

Then the big news hit: ABC News initially reported that an FBI manhunt was under way to get Mark Koernke in connection with the bombing. Earlier that afternoon, Koernke reportedly fled his Dexter, Michigan, home with a trunk full of rifles. ABC described McVeigh and Nichols as disciples of Koernke's "hate-filled espousal of armed defiance of the government."

Koernke had faxed militia-friendly Congressman Steve Stockman (R-Texas) a cryptic notice on the bombing that read, "First update. Bldg 7 to 10 floors only. Military people on scene—BATF/FBI. Bomb threat received last week. Perpetrator unknown at this time. Oklahoma." The time-stamp on top of the fax indicated that the message was sent at 8:59 A.M. from a Michigan number. That would have been 7:59 Oklahoma time—a full hour before the blast. Investigators didn't get the fax right away because

Stockman's first response was to forward it to the National Rifle Association and not the FBI.

Then came a second damning report: A man named McVeigh was widely reported to have served as a bodyguard for Koernke on a recent speaking tour through Florida.

The press zoomed in on Koernke. They dug out his videotapes and pulled out his most extreme statements. In one widely repeated segment, Koernke holds a coil of rope in his left hand and says, "I did some basic math the other day. I found that using the old-style math, you can get about four politicians for about a hundred and twenty feet of rope. . . . Remember: When you use this stuff, always try and find a willow tree. The entertainment will last longer."

Koernke, and with him the entire militia movement, was vilified as the "new political monster" that *Time* magazine blamed for the horrific bombing in Oklahoma City.

But the ABC report was wrong. FBI director Louis Freeh announced the next day that neither the Michigan Militia nor Koernke was suspected in connection with the bombing. In fact, both had been under investigation since the Camp Grayling incident two months earlier, when a faction of the Michigan Militia, which may have been incited by Koernke's presentation at a public meeting of the Militia, allegedly plotted to blow up a National Guard base.

Soon after that Koernke himself emerged, showing up for work as a maintenance worker at the University of Michigan. He brushed off reporters' questions and didn't seem a bit concerned about the controversy that had swirled around him. In part, Koernke had been the victim of a comedy of errors. The time stamp on his fax to Congressman Stockman seemed to prove that he knew about the bombing *before* it happened. In fact, the clock on the fax machine had been wrong. As for the man named McVeigh who reportedly served as Koernke's bodyguard, he didn't really exist. The man who had traveled with Koernke through Florida was named McKay, not McVeigh.

But the demonization of the militia movement continued as the horror of Oklahoma City was tied to the militias in countless news stories and powerful images broadcast across the country and throughout the world. The antimilitia sentiment quickly reached Washington, D.C., where lawmakers called for tough measures against paramilitary groups. Congressmen in both parties rushed to endorse antiterrorism legislation that would give broad new powers to federal agencies (including the FBI and the Bureau of Alcohol, Tobacco, and Firearms) to investigate and infiltrate militias. Most of the legislation, including President Clinton's antiterrorism bill, had already been proposed, but was going nowhere in Congress. With the Oklahoma bombing, these bills came to the forefront, winning broad bipartisan support.

An even more intense wave of paranoia struck the militias. It became a virtual article of faith that the bombing was the work of people within the federal government. The purpose, many believed, was threefold: (1) to demonize the militias; (2) to provide an excuse to give federal agencies even more power; and (3) to set the stage for a violent crackdown on militia members and other gun owners.

In fact, several militia leaders had predicted the scenario even before the bombing. In the video *Invasion & Betrayal,* which was made several months before the bombing, Militia of Montana spokesman

Bob Fletcher said: "Watch and you will see an increased amount of terroristic activities pick up here in America. Now, you watch, they will try and pin this on the militia/patriot movement." Three weeks before the bombing, Texas militia leader Jon Roland sent out a national communiqué warning, "We have several reports of possible plans for atrocities to be committed by [federal] agents against innocent persons and blamed on militia activists." Among the "atrocity targets," Roland had warned, were "crowded public places, to be bombed and the bombings blamed on militia leaders, with evidence to later be planted on them."

"So it comes to pass," the Militia of Montana declared after the bombing in its newsletter, *Taking Aim*. "The terrorist activity did take place and they are doing everything in their power, through their media tools, to pin this on the militia/patriot movement."

In a thoughtful statement entitled "A Time for Understanding," Roland expressed "outrage and sadness" over the "atrocity in Oklahoma City" and urged a thorough investigation. He warned that the natural desire for retribution could obscure "the most important lessons we can learn from this tragedy."

"Assuming for a moment that this was the act of a few aggrieved individuals," Roland wrote, "we need to consider the factors that lead persons to commit acts of terrorism." What pushes such individuals over the edge, he said, is having their concerns ignored.

"The aggrieved can forgive anything but being ignored," Roland wrote, "and we live in a time when the aggrieved can be very dangerous."

That said, Roland added his voice to the many speculating that the bombing was the work of the federal government: "We don't know all the facts yet, but we should consider that this atrocity may be another Reichstag fire, staged by parties within the government for political effect."

The Reichstag fire Roland referred to was the 1933 burning of the German parliament building in Berlin. The fire was set by Nazi loyalists but blamed on Hitler's enemies. As the flames engulfed the building, Hitler shouted, "It's the Communists!" In the days and weeks that followed, Hitler commenced a ruthless crackdown on his political opposition, did away with the last remnants of German democracy, and solidified Nazi domination of the country. As he toured the wreckage left behind by the fire, Hitler declared, "You are witnessing the beginning of a great epoch in German history. This fire is the beginning." The day after the fire, Hitler issued an emergency decree that he said was necessary to protect the country from further acts of terrorism. The decree suspended many of the rights guaranteed by the German constitution, including free speech, free press, secrecy of mail and telephone conversations, and the right to assemble. Historian John Toland describes what happened next:

The emergency measures that followed, designed primarily to put down a non-existent revolt, turned out to be a leap forward in Hitler's drive for total power. Truckloads of SA and SS men [military personnel] hastily sworn in as auxiliaries were helping the police enforce the decree. They descended on the rooms and taverns of known Reds and carted them off to prison or interrogations cellars.

> More than three thousand Communists
> and Social Democrats were taken into
> protective custody by the regular police.
> Airdromes and ports were under strict
> surveillance while trains were searched at
> frontiers.[1]

This was precisely the vision Roland and many
other militia members feared: a replay of 1933
Germany in 1995 America.

In the weeks that followed the Oklahoma bombing, militia members all over the country began calling the attack "Clinton's Reichstag fire." They
compared antiterrorist legislation—which called for
expanded wiretapping authority, an easing of the
ban on using the military in domestic law enforcement, and other measures that civil libertarians
said curtailed rights—with Hitler's emergency
decree. There was plenty of noise on Capitol Hill to
fuel the paranoia. Senator Kay Bailey Hutchison (R-
Texas), for example, told *Time* magazine, "I think
Americans should get used to a little lessening of our
freedoms."

Clinton clinched the Reichstag comparison for
many on May 5 with a speech in East Lansing,
Michigan. Speaking about the Oklahoma bombing, he
lashed out at the militias. "If you appropriate our
sacred symbols for paranoid purposes and compare
yourselves to colonial militias who fought for the
democracy you now rail against, you are wrong,"
Clinton said in a commencement address at Michigan
State University. "How dare you suggest that we in

---

[1] John Toland, *Adolf Hitler* (New York: Doubleday and
Company, Inc.), pp. 301–2.

the freest nation on earth live in tyranny? How dare you call yourselves patriots and heroes?"

For militia members, Clinton's words echoed Hitler's when he pointed to the Reichstag fire and shouted, "The Communists did it!" Only this time it was the militias who were blamed.

AFTER OKLAHOMA

The dogmas of the quiet past are inadequate to the stormy present. The occasion is piled high with difficulty, and we must rise with the occasion. As our case is new, so must we act anew.

—*Abraham Lincoln*

It's Sunday morning in an auction barn four miles south of Wolverine, Michigan. Thirty people patiently wait in the rows of plastic chairs on the barn's concrete floor.

The assembled have Bibles. Some of them also have guns by their sides. The men wear battle fatigues. A preacher arrives and proudly stands before his parishioners. He wears a military camouflage uniform that bears his secular rank in thick black capital letters: *COMMANDER*.

Welcome to Freedom Church. Your pastor is Norman Olson, the founder of the Michigan Militia.

"God's hand of judgment is going to sweep across this nation," Olson says, his deep voice laced with a mix of reverence and urgency. "We've got precious little time left. We've got to make up our minds.

'Choose ye today who ye will serve.' The day of the Lord is at hand."

Prayer will no longer be enough, Olson tells the congregation. "For the last thirty years, the church has been praying, 'God heal this land, God heal this land.' But the church and the Christians of this country haven't done anything about it. They've done a lot of praying, but if God only wanted people to pray, he would have created brains on a plate! He made people with backbones and arms and feet to do things.

"Now the question is this," Olson says, lowering his voice. "Is this constitutional Christian militia of America the answer to thirty years of prayer? I believe it is. And if this is the answer to thirty years of prayer, nothing, nothing, nothing is going to stop this work we've begun." The parishioners nod in approval.

Freedom Church is just one sign that the militia movement has entered a new phase: After Oklahoma.

The trauma resulting from the deadliest terrorist attack in American history has caused a radical transformation in the movement. It has affected militias in dramatically different ways. Some have lost members or closed down. Others have grown, and it is clear that, on a national scale, militia membership has increased significantly. The messages of the militias have changed in different ways, too. Some of the groups have moderated their rhetoric, while others have grown more radical. The transformation continues; the movement will never be the same.

The once-obscure phenomenon of self-styled patriots preparing for war has now been front-page news in every major newspaper in America. The movement's once-unknown leaders have faced off on national television against the likes of Ted Koppel,

Sam Donaldson, Dan Rather, and Phil Donahue. They have been the subject of speeches by the President of the United States. Countless media reports have associated the militias with the horror of the Oklahoma bombing.

Norm Olson now preaches at Freedom Church because he was forced out of Calvary Baptist, where he had been pastor for five years. For the parishioners at Calvary Baptist, the Oklahoma bombing brought too much attention to their pastor's militia activities. They complained that Olson and deacon Ray Southwell were turning their small-town house of worship into a militia stronghold. Olson and Southwell left to start their own church—one that Olson says isn't afraid to defend freedom.

Within a week of the bombing, another prominent militiaman from Michigan lost his job. Mark Koernke's shortwave radio show, *The Intelligence Report,* was yanked off the air by World Wide Christian Radio (WWCR), which had broadcast it for an eventful seven months. WWCR continued to broadcast several other militia-related programs, but Koernke's was pulled. "We've got to get the gasoline off the fires," said station general manager George McClintock. But a resourceful and determined Koernke managed to get the show going again, broadcasting via satellite and getting over one hundred AM and FM stations to carry his program.

Less then two weeks after the bombing, a leadership crisis struck the Michigan Militia. Militia members voted to oust Norm Olson and Ray Southwell from their leadership positions after the two released a statement many militia members found outrageous. The April statement sent out to the national media by Olson and Southwell read, "The wrath of the country has been directed toward the great men and women of the Michigan Militia. Now here's the truth: On April 19, 1995, a day that will live in infamy, the government of Japan, in retaliation for the United States gas attack on the subway in Japan, blew up the federal building in Oklahoma City."

Egged on by California conspiracy researcher Debra von Trapp, Olson and Southwell claimed the Oklahoma bombing was the latest act in an undeclared and secret war between the United States and Japan. Most militia members found the theory preposterous, although many believed the U.S. government was somehow involved in the bombing. Removed from their leadership positions, Olson and Southwell remained active in the group.

But several other militias around the country did not fare so well.

In New York, the state's first and largest militia voted to disband after the bombing. The Orange County Constitutional Militia, which had claimed a membership of more than 150, regrouped under the name Orange County Committee of Correspondence. The new organization did without uniforms and military training. The name "Committee of Correspondence" was taken from the groups of colonists that formed in the 1760s and 1770s to organize political opposition to taxes imposed by England.

Several other militias also disbanded, including California's Butte County Militia. Former militia commander Don Illa said that membership fell after the bombing as friends and family members pressured militia members to drop out. Founded in February 1995, the group had reached a membership of 180 before the bombing. Illa released a statement announcing the decision to disband:

The Butte County Militia was formed for the noble cause of defending our constitutionally guaranteed rights. It was believed that the general populace favored such an idea, but the established media has somehow managed to demonize this honorable institution.

The members of the Butte County Militia, after several meetings and careful deliberation, have come to the following conclusions:

That the basic definition of the word "militia" describes an armed group of people.

That because of the unwarranted fears generated locally about an armed militia training in Butte County, the Butte County Militia assumed the posture of an unarmed group. After all, it was a public entity and was answerable to the dictates of the people.

This posture, however, contradicts the definition of the word "militia" and in reality indicates that the Butte County Militia exists in name only.

That we, therefore, officially abandon this title.

As with the Orange County Constitutional Militia, Illa said a nonparamilitary group would emerge to take the militia's place. The new group would be strictly political and educational.

But the fate of the Butte County and Orange County militias was the exception to the rule. Overall, the movement, fueled by national media attention,

grew dramatically in the months following the
Oklahoma bombing.

In a national survey of militia activity one month
after the bombing, the Anti-Defamation League
(ADL) concluded, "Militia gains plainly appear to
outweigh losses—contrary to the widespread expecta-
tion that public shock and revulsion at the bombing
might prompt the militias to disband."

The ADL report, entitled "Beyond the Bombing:
The Militia Menace Grows," documented militia organizations in forty states and estimated membership at
fifteen thousand. In California alone, the report
located thirty militia groups, stretching from San
Diego to the Oregon border. The ADL attributed
much of the militia movement's growth to "an effec-
tive communications network."

Militia leaders agreed that the movement grew
after the bombing and claimed that militias had now
formed in all fifty states. Texas militiaman Jon Roland
estimated that nationally more than half a million
Americans were involved in militias, while other militia leaders put the number at more than a million.

The primary reason that the Oklahoma attack
didn't cause militias to disband was the widespread
belief among militia members that the government
itself was behind it. The bombing spawned a cottage
industry of conspiracy researchers who desperately
sought out clues linking the federal government to the
terror attack. Computer and fax networks buzzed
with "intelligence reports" poking holes in the government's version of the bombing. Militia leaders began
referring to the prime bombing suspect as "Lee
Harvey McVeigh," a reference to the accused assassin
of President John F. Kennedy. Polls have consistently
shown that millions of Americans do not believe that

Lee Harvey Oswald was the lone assassin of President Kennedy, and militia leaders predict the American public will eventually view the official explanation of the Oklahoma bombing with the same skepticism.

One of the first "clues" to make the militia circuit was a seismograph reading from the Oklahoma Geological Survey, located twenty miles from the bomb site. At approximately 9:02 A.M. on April 19, 1995, the Survey recorded two distinct seismic blips separated by ten seconds. To conspiracy researchers, this provided irrefutable evidence that there were two bombs, not the single truck bomb allegedly planted by Timothy McVeigh.

The seismograph readings were legitimate, but investigators attributed the second blip to the tremendous impact of the building collapsing after the truck bomb exploded. Conspiracy researchers dismissed this explanation and continued their investigations, sending out daily updates through various militia communications networks.

The researchers received support from several former government investigators, including Ted Gunderson, the former head of the FBI office in Los Angeles. Gunderson sent letters to several U.S. senators maintaining that a truck fertilizer bomb could not have destroyed the building. Benton Partin, a retired Air Force brigadier general, agreed. Partin, who is a chemical expert with thirty-one years of active-duty experience, wrote a six-page letter to Oklahoma senator Donald Nickles alleging that FBI investigators were engaging in a massive cover-up.

The frenzied work of the conspiracy researchers prompted Oklahoma legislator Charles Key to call for an independent state investigation into the bombing. "I am convinced that the government is not being forthright about the kind of bomb(s), the number of explosions, the placement of the explosives and other crucial aspects of the April 19th bombing," Key said in a statement issued on June 28. "Those who are challenging the current bombing explanation are highly credible and have impeccable credentials regarding explosives, munitions, and covert intelligence."

On June 15, 1995, the militia movement reached another milestone: testifying before the United States Senate.

At a raucous Senate hearing full of conspiracy theories and ominous talk of revolution, militia leaders warned of civil war in America if antiterrorism and gun-control legislation becomes law. They spoke beneath a colossal Senate seal in one of largest hearing rooms on Capitol Hill.

"If the truth is not told, Congress will pass legislation that will lead us to civil war," Michigan militiaman Ray Southwell said after the sometimes surreal hearing. The standing-room-only crowd included dozens of militia supporters, some with toddlers in tow.

Mark Koernke and his associate John Stadtmiller sat in the front row as the senators grilled the five militiamen who testified: John Trochmann (Montana), Bob Fletcher (Montana), James Johnson (Ohio), Norm Olson (Michigan), and Ken Adams (Michigan). Koernke and Stadtmiller had just driven twenty-two hours from Michigan, stopping only for food and gas. They arrived in Washington less than an hour before the start of the hearing, expecting that Koernke would testify.

Senate staffers said Koernke was invited to testify,

but that they did not know he had arrived when the militia panel was called before the committee.

Stadtmiller smelled conspiracy. "I think there are powerful people here who didn't want Mark to testify."

Koernke didn't seem bothered. He just sat silently in the front row, taking pages and pages of notes.

James Johnson set the tone for the hearing, warning the senators, "The only thing standing between some of the current legislation that is being contemplated and armed conflict is time."

He said the hearings offered a ray of hope, however. "It's good that we are getting these views aired out, because two hundred years ago the British didn't get the hint until they saw dead redcoats out there."

The hearing before the Senate subcommittee on terrorism was sponsored by Senator Arlen Specter (R-Pennsylvania), who billed the event as an attempt to determine whether militias "represent a clear and present danger" to the country. But in reality, the Militia of Montana had written to Specter more than a month earlier to ask for the hearing.

"We wanted a chance to respond to all the lies people were saying about us," explained John Trochmann.

The militia leaders again denounced the Oklahoma bombing and defended their movement as patriotic and defensive in nature. Instead, they insisted, it is the government that is guilty of "corruption, tyranny, and oppression."

"In short, the federal government needs a good spanking to make it behave," said Norm Olson, who wore military fatigues sporting the rank *COMMANDER*.

During the question-and-answer period, Olson and Specter engaged in several heated exchanges. One argument ensued after Olson took issue with a flyer in the hands of Senator Herb Kohl, who was sitting next to Senator Specter. The flyer showed a picture of Adolf Hitler with his stiff-armed salute and the caption, "All in favor of gun control raise your right hand." Olson pointed out that the picture was not the work of a militia group but a copyrighted poster by the gun-rights group Jews for the Preservation of Firearms Ownership. (Olson, in fact, was right.) Specter seized on the comment as a sign of anti-Semitism.

Specter: Well, we'll pick up your comments about copyright, and about Jews, in a few minutes—

Olson: No, sir. I believe you are trying to lay at the feet of the militia some culpability. . . . You're trying to make us out to be something we are not, much like the press has tried to do over this last year. But we are not what you think we are. We are not what the press wants to feed to the American public. We are people who are opposed—opposed—to racism, hatred. We are people who love our government, our Constitution. . . . What we stand against is corruption. We stand against oppression and tyranny in government. We, many of us, are coming to the conclusion that you best represent that corruption and tyranny. . . .

Specter: Well, I'm not going to interrupt you in any of your responses—

Olson: And I'm not going to keep on preaching. Go ahead.

Specter: But I am going to note that you are interrupting me when I start to say to you that we will get back to your statement about copyright and about Jews. We'll get back to that. What I want to get back to this moment is your statement about retribution and violence as an apparent justification for—

Olson: Just let me—

Specter: Now, wait a minute! I'm not going to let you interrupt me again. What I want to come to, I want to have a full discussion with you, Mr. Olson. Because I want your ideas fully exposed. And the reason—

Olson: There are other people on the panel that deserve a chance to speak.

Specter: I know. But I'm the chairman, and they'll have a chance to speak. And I'm not going to interrupt you at all, whenever you start to reply. And what I want to do is, I want to hear all your ideas. Because I want your ideas compared to mine. And I want to let the American public judge whether you're right or I'm right. . . . And I don't take lightly your comment that I represent corruption. I don't take that lightly at all. And I want you to prove it, if you are going to say that.

Specter also hammered Olson on comments he made to Lesley Stahl of CBS News shortly after the Oklahoma bombing. Olson told Stahl that he could understand how somebody could become angry enough to make a terrorist attack.

Specter: I cannot understand how anybody can understand why someone would bomb the Oklahoma federal building as a matter of retribution.

Olson: Then you don't understand the problem we've had in Northern Ireland. You don't understand the problem we've had in South Africa. You don't understand the hatred, the retaliation, the revenge that has been going on around this globe since time immemorial. Then you don't understand the dynamic.

Specter: Well, Mr. Olson, I may not understand. And that is why we've had these hearings, so that you can have the full opportunity to express yourself.

The hearings also provided an airing for some popular militia conspiracy theories, as the senators found themselves accused in the plot to undermine freedom in the United States.

"I submit to you, sir, that the Central Intelligence Agency has been in the business of killing Americans and killing people in the United States and around the world since 1946. The Central Intelligence Agency is the grandest conspirator behind all this government," testified Olson. "Perhaps its puppeteer strings even reach to the senators before us today."

Olson presented the Senate committee with a hefty three-ring binder packed with more than eight hundred pages of documents he said proved a far-reaching conspiracy to undermine the U.S. Constitution and deprive Americans of basic rights. The binder included a seventy-five-page section alleging a government conspiracy to cover up the truth about who bombed the federal building in Oklahoma City.

C-SPAN broadcast the hearings four times during the next week. Militia leaders were given less than two hours before the senators, but they considered it a victory. In the words of the *Washington Post,* the militiamen "did not back down in the face of their questioners. It could be said they gave as good as they got—especially if one believes their accusations that the United States is engaged in diabolical conspiracies."

New York Democrat Charles Schumer denounced Specter for providing "a soapbox for the wacky right," but the senator defended the hearings. "A public hearing of grievances that the citizens have is a very useful and healthy thing."

Senator Specter is surely right, but the hearings did further raise the visibility of the militias and help them to attract new members.

> **T**hose who would give up essential liberty to purchase safety deserve neither liberty nor safety.
>
> —*Benjamin Franklin*

CONCLUSION 12

> **I** think Americans should get used to a little lessening of our freedoms.
>
> —*Texas senator Kay Bailey Hutchison, shortly after the Oklahoma City bombing*

At 2:30 A.M. on June 28, 1995, police sergeant Matt May gripped his 9-mm semiautomatic pistol, took aim, and pulled the trigger four times. He hit his target with deadly precision.

One shot shattered Ohio militiaman Michael Hill's skull. Another hit him in the chest, a third grazed his shoulder and his cheek, and the fourth sailed past its target. Michael Hill died instantly—the Ohio Unorganized Militia's first casualty.

Twenty-five years earlier, Hill had been one of the Ohio National Guardsmen who battled antiwar protesters at Kent State University. The Guardsmen opened fire on the protesters, killing four unarmed students.

The Kent State incident shocked the nation and became a rallying cry for a generation of political activists. Hill wrote a book, *I Was There: What Really Happened at Kent State,* that put most of the blame on the protesters. But a protest song by Neil Young helped turn the incident into a lasting symbol of the deadly abuse of power by government.

> This summer I hear the drumming
> Four dead in Ohio

This time the fifty-year-old Hill was on the other side of the law's deadly use of force. Hill's fateful encounter with Sergeant May began at 2:15 A.M. as he drove his 1972 AMC Ambassador eastbound on Ohio Highway 16; he was going home from a militia meeting in the town of Brice. May had good reason to pull Hill over. His car had no license plate, only a hand-crafted sign that read *MILITIA CHAPLAIN 3–13.* A chaplain and colonel in the Ohio Unorganized Militia, Hill believed the state had no right to require him to register his car.

Sergeant May flipped on his siren and lights, and Hill pulled his clunky gas guzzler over to the side of the road. When Hill got out of his car, May ordered him to get back inside. Hill got back in his car and, instead of waiting for the officer, started driving again. May pulled him over a second time, and Hill, this time bearing a .45 caliber handgun, again got out and started walking toward the police car.

It was then that May fired the fatal four shots.

Sergeant May called the shooting self-defense, charging that Hill had drawn his gun and was preparing to fire it. Hill also had a loaded assault rifle in the trunk of his car. But three other militiamen who say they witnessed the incident insist Hill never drew his gun and charge that May fired without cause. The men, who say they were driving behind Hill, filed sworn affidavits with the FBI and the county sheriff's department. But Sheriff Bernard Gibson has called the witnesses' story bogus.

This much is undisputed by both the witnesses and the police:

- Hill did not have state-issued license plates.

- Hill was armed as he left the car.

- Hill did not fire a single shot.

- Officer May's gunshots killed Hill.

As of this writing, a formal investigation of the incident is under way by Muskingum County, and Michael Hill's widow, Arlene, has filed a civil lawsuit against Sergeant May and the sheriff's department.

Sergeant May, twenty-four years old, wasn't yet born when Hill stood with the Ohio National Guard as they opened fire on antiwar protesters at Kent State. But militia members across the nation viewed his gunshots in the same way antiwar protesters viewed the shots fired by the National Guard at Kent State on May 4, 1970. The Hill shooting got limited media coverage outside of Ohio, but it was the biggest story since the Oklahoma bombing in the alternative militia media of fax networks, shortwave radio shows, Internet newsgroups, and underground newsletters. The Hill shooting was another rallying cry, another example of what the militias say they were fighting against.

"I hope that shooting militia members by law enforcement officials has not become a sporting event," said Michigan militiaman Ken Adams, who flew to Ohio to help Hill's widow prepare a legal response to the shooting. Adams helped Arlene Hill obtain the pro bono legal services of libertarian lawyer Nancy Lord; at the same time, Ohio militia members were calling the shooting "cold-blooded murder."

Of course, the shooting of Michael Hill was not another Kent State. The student victims in 1970 were unarmed and protesting a war that millions of Americans thought was wrong. Hill was approaching a police officer with a loaded .45 caliber gun after driving without license plates in the strange belief that the state has no right to require car registration. That doesn't mean he deserved to die, but he was not a blameless victim.

Sergeant May might sincerely believe he acted in self-defense, especially because so much media coverage has painted militia members as heavily armed terrorists bent on overthrowing the government. It's not hard to understand why the militia sign on the back of Hill's car would spook a twenty-four-year-old police officer on patrol at 2:30 A.M. But by repeatedly pulling the trigger of his 9-mm pistol, Sergeant May gave the militia movement a martyr. The surest way to fuel the growth of citizens' militias is to give them martyrs. The movement is full of leaders who seem to think it is their destiny to be a martyr to their cause.

The Ohio incident is a warning: We overestimate the militia threat at our own peril. The sight of grown men dressed in military fatigues and marching in the woods with assault rifles is frightening to most

Americans. The rhetoric of militia leaders is often belligerent and extreme. And the extent of the media coverage lavished on militias seems to say, "Watch out! There's a militiaman with an AK–47 assault rifle under your bed!" We need a reality check. Even as we study and watch the militia movement, we need to remember two things.

First, the movement is small. The most reliable estimates put membership in citizens' militias at between fifteen thousand and a hundred thousand. And even these figures overstate their strength, because the militias are independent organizations operating on a local level. Militia members communicate nationally through a sophisticated alternative media, but their communications reflect a rancorous difference of opinion more than a unity of purpose. Organizationally, there is no significant structure on the national level.

Second, the overwhelming majority of militia members are harmless. They are often angry and disillusioned, but they are dedicated to self-defense. The danger lies in the brooding and mentally unstable loner who is too paranoid even to join a militia or other group. With the wide availability of bomb-making material and know-how, the danger of the violent fanatic is real, but it is a danger that has little to do with the existence of citizens' militias.

The more serious cause for concern is the deeper, more widespread discontent and uneasiness the militias represent. Militias are a symptom of a much larger problem facing American society. We face a crisis of confidence in our democratic system of government, and it is a crisis that has been caused largely by the irresponsibility of our political leaders.

The rantings of conspiracy theorists can easily be

dismissed, but distrust of our federal government
extends far beyond the tiny minority that believes the
paranoid fanatics of the far right and far left. A
CNN/*USA Today* poll conducted in May 1995
revealed the depth of the problem: 39 percent of those
surveyed "say the federal government has become so
large and so powerful it poses an immediate threat to
the rights and freedoms of ordinary citizens." There is
something wrong when even a small minority of the
population feels this way, but when two out of every
five Americans say they fear their own government,
the problem is approaching crisis levels.

And the feeling transcends political distinctions.
Democrats, Republicans, and independents
responded to the poll in almost identical numbers.
"People of both left and right have the same fear of
too much government," University of Alabama professor Brent Smith told *USA Today.* "They're coming
from different ends of the earth, yet their fear is federal government intrusion."

In this context, the worst response to the militia
movement—and to the Oklahoma bombing—is new
antiterrorism measures that put even more power into
the hands of federal law enforcement. In the months
following the bombing, a bipartisan consensus
emerged in Congress: To combat domestic terrorism,
we may have to sacrifice some of our rights.

President Clinton's antiterrorism proposal, which
received broad bipartisan support, called for hiring a
thousand federal agents, boosting the budget of the
Bureau of Alcohol, Tobacco, and Firearms by $20
million a year, making it easier for federal investigators to place wiretaps on people's phones, and allowing the military to assist in domestic law enforcement.
The last provision is the most disturbing. Since 1878,

following the bloodbath of the Civil War and the chaos of Reconstruction, Congress has banned the military from enforcing civilian law. Indeed, one of the hallmarks of democratic governments is that they don't use the military against their own citizens.

Measures such as President Clinton's antiterrorism bill and its Republican-sponsored counterparts serve only to inflame the paranoia of the militias, but what is more disturbing is that they give more power to the federal government at a time when we should be scaling that power back.

The surest way to defuse the militia movement is to show that the fears of those attracted to it are unfounded. Trying to disprove the paranoid fantasies of people such as Mark Koernke is a waste of time; the intensely conspiratorial mind-set will always exist on the political fringes, but we can address the more widespread discontent in America that drives people toward the peddlers of paranoia. One step in that direction is greater openness. Conspiracy theorists thrive on ignorance, not information.

The *New York Times* calls the federal raids on Randy Weaver at Ruby Ridge, Idaho, in 1992 and on the Branch Davidians at Waco, Texas, in 1993 "two of the biggest law enforcement fiascoes in recent memory." They are also two primary reasons for the growth of the militia movement. And both fiascoes have been compounded by government secrecy and the unwillingness to hold anyone responsible for deadly mistakes. In fact, Larry Potts, the lead FBI officer at Ruby Ridge and Waco, was actually *promoted* to the number two spot in the agency after the Waco debacle. By August 1995, three years after the Ruby Ridge standoff, public pressure finally forced FBI Director Louis Freeh to suspend Potts.

There is a feeling among some federal officials that investigating Waco and Ruby Ridge only rewards extremists in the militia movement. It is true that extremist crackpots have used the incidents for their own purposes, but that doesn't absolve federal agencies from taking responsibility for their actions.

The Clinton Administration has actively worked to blunt investigation into Waco and Ruby Ridge (even though the Weaver incident took place under the Bush Administration). In a July 5, 1995, letter to the Congressional subcommittee planning hearings on Waco, Treasury Secretary Robert Rubin wrote, "I am worried that investigating events at Waco, without investigating the extreme activities of some militias, seems to suggest that law enforcement agencies are the real threat to the safety of American citizens."

Rubin argued that the hearings might damage public confidence in federal law enforcement agents. "Some," Rubin warned, "may try to use these hearings to serve another agenda: to erode public support for federal firearms laws."

Rubin's approach is woefully misguided. Democratic government depends on openness and accountability. Investigations won't convince the most hard-core conspiracy theorists, but they may help restore faith in our democratic system among the much larger segment of the population that has come to distrust our government.

The danger of terrorism is still real and growing, but its sources are far more widespread and difficult to pin down than citizens' militias. In 1983 there were 442 bombings in the United States. By 1993 there were 1,880. And the bombs have grown larger and deadlier. They are made with substances as crude and readily available as fertilizer. For nearly two decades, the Unabomber has manufactured mail bombs out of scrap metal. His mailings have killed four people, maimed and terrorized several others, and demonstrated that he, or any other brilliantly deranged killer, can do tremendous damage. The Unabomber's motivating philosophy is a mix of radical environmentalism and anarchism; it has nothing to do with the militias. As the FBI has tried to hunt him down, his bombs have become smaller, more sophisticated, and deadlier.

If the federal government banned militias tomorrow and draconian antiterrorism legislation became law, we would still live with the threat of domestic terrorism. We would just have fewer rights.

INDEX

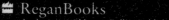